Starting a Business Roadmap

The Beginner Entrepreneur's Guide to Be Your Own Boss, Leverage AI, and Achieve Financial Independence

Russel Grant

Contents

Cheat Sheet   IV

Introduction   1

1. The Power of the Entrepreneurial Mindset   4

2. Building a Strong Foundation   19

3. Launching with Confidence   35

4. Mastering Digital Marketing and Brand Power   55

5. Smart Money Moves   80

6. Scaling to New Heights   96

7. Seizing New Market Opportunities   109

8. The Future with AI   124

Conclusion   140

References   143

GET YOUR FREE
PROMPT ENGINEERING
CHEAT SHEET!

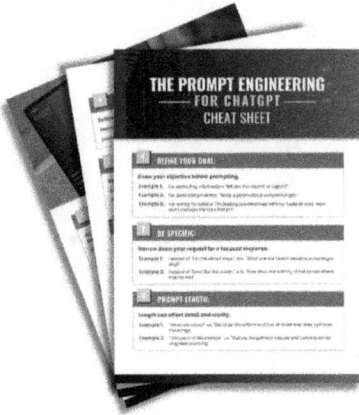

SCAN ME

Go to the address below,
or scan the code.

https://cheatsheet.tips

Introduction

Everyone has an idea, but the world belongs to those who execute –
Unknown

D o you have a million-dollar idea?

Chances are, you do. Every day, countless individuals are struck with brilliant concepts, innovative solutions, and groundbreaking products. But here's the harsh reality: ideas are cheap. It's the execution that separates the dreamers from the doers.

I guess this is the story of all entrepreneurs. As a group that has embarked on a mission to build a life for itself, we spot ideas all around us. Robberies in banks are increasing at an alarming rate. Maybe I should build a business around safety devices. People are becoming vegan. Maybe I should start a vegan bakery business.

Unfortunately, that "maybe" never turns into a reality. We get caught up in our daily struggles, and that "maybe" slips away into the sea of lost dreams.

Something similar happened to me when I was in my first job. I landed a job straight out of college and at a small business in my town. It wasn't very well known, but it was profitable. The owner-cum-manager was a nice guy and was handling his business well.

But the 20-year-old I wanted to contribute in more ways than what I was hired for. Besides keeping account of the day-to-day operation, I wanted to experiment and innovate. My brain will continually conjure up ideas that I think would help the business.

But every time I'd bring up a new idea to my boss, it was clear he wasn't interested. He'd give a polite nod, but I could tell from his expression that he found my suggestions more annoying than helpful. In a way, I understood. Here I was, a recent graduate, trying to change a company he'd built over the years. Still, I couldn't help but feel deflated. Without new growth, there wasn't much room for my own ambitions.

As I said, you get stuck in your daily struggles, and that maybe slips into the sea of crushed dreams.

You see, the world isn't kind to idle minds. It rewards action, persistence, and the relentless pursuit of goals. It's not enough to merely think big; you must do big.

After a series of refusals from my boss, I knew I had to quit and do something on my own. And that's what I did. Since then, I have started multiple businesses, some of which did million of dollars a year in revenue. It was all blood, sweat and tears.

Thankfully, there's some good news. The good news is you don't have to work as hard as me or the entrepreneurs of my time to taste success. Today, you have more capabilities at your disposal to launch a business with less effort. That's because of the AI revolution.

Artificial Intelligence (AI), once a concept confined to the realm of science fiction, is now a tangible force reshaping industries and economies. It's now up to a point where it's no longer hype. It's a technological marvel capable of learning, reasoning, and making decisions. For business owners, AI is the modern-day alchemist, transforming data into gold.

AI is like having a super smart assistant. It can do all sorts of cool stuff, like helping you understand your customers better. It can analyze their buying habits, what they like, and what they don't. This helps you tailor your products and services to their exact needs. It's like having a mind reader!

AI can also automate a lot of boring tasks. Imagine your computer doing all the data entry, sending out emails, and scheduling meetings. This frees up your time to focus on the fun stuff, like coming up with new ideas and building relationships with your customers.

But that's not all! AI can even help you make smarter decisions. It can crunch numbers, analyze trends, and predict what might happen in the future. This helps you stay ahead of the curve and make choices that will benefit your business. And you're about to learn it all in the chapters that follow.

Each chapter is divided into two sections. The first section is about the basic concepts of business, and the second pertains to using AI to carry out tasks.

But that's not where you start building a business. You start at the very bottom, which is the foundation. The second chapter is where you'll learn how to build a strong foundation for your business. And yes, we'll be using AI for it.

In Chapter 4, we'll be learning another important concept: marketing. This is one of the most crucial aspects of running a business. My father recalls the hard days when the only way to advertise – at least for small businesses -- was to go from door to door and distribute pamphlets. Mid-size businesses could afford to place ads in newspapers or magazines.

But thankfully, you won't have to go through that trouble. In today's times, you can run ads from your home that too within half the price. With the use of AI, this gets even simpler.

The second part of the book, we explore how to scale your business and seize new opportunities. At some point, scaling becomes inevitable. I'll show the exact steps I've taken to scale my businesses from scratch to record success.

Then, we'll close with the future outlook for AI, which will help you prepare for the AI revolution and make your business AI-ready.

By the end, you'll have a deep knowledge of building a business and using AI in the process. While there are no guarantees, you can surely taste success like tens of hundreds of people who have taken up this book.

That being said, let's get started and build your business from ground zero.

Chapter One

The Power of the Entrepreneurial Mindset

Being an entrepreneur is more than just starting a business; it's about embracing a mindset that sees every turn and every event as an opportunity. This mindset is resilient and focused, always working towards a goal despite the obstacles that may arise.

Imagine it like climbing a mountain: reaching the peak isn't just about wanting it badly enough or even having the best tools and equipment. It requires so much more. You need a deep understanding of the terrain, the knowledge to navigate challenges, the right resources, and the mental and physical strength to push forward. Above all, you must possess the will to adapt to the ever-changing environment around you.

The entrepreneurial journey is much the same. The path to building a successful business can feel daunting, much like scaling a towering mountain. However, the moment you start taking those first small steps, the road ahead becomes clearer. And remember, you don't have to climb this mountain alone. Seek guidance, ask for help, and always be open to learning and adapting along the way. Embrace the journey with curiosity and determination, knowing that each step brings you closer to your goal.

This book aims to equip you with the confidence and resources you need to start living your entrepreneurial dreams. With the right mindset, there are no limits to what you can achieve. Keep your eyes on the summit, stay resilient, and trust in your ability to overcome any challenge that comes your way.

Developing the Entrepreneurial Spirit and Overcoming Fears

Becoming an entrepreneur is less about unbroken success and more about cultivating a resilient, entrepreneurial spirit. Few entrepreneurs can boast of an unblemished winning streak. In reality, most successful entrepreneurs have encountered more failures than successes.

These setbacks are not signs of defeat but rather stepping stones to greater achievements. Take Milton Hershey, who faced three failed candy businesses before he found monumental success with his eponymous chocolate company.

Bill Gates experienced a significant failure with his first company. Steve Jobs was famously ousted from Apple, the company he co-founded, before making a triumphant return through another venture. Even Walt Disney was fired from a job for not being "creative enough." Every entrepreneur has a journey marked with failures, often more numerous than their successes.

What sets these entrepreneurs apart is their ability to develop an unbreakable spirit and to rise again after every fall. So, what fears are holding you back from taking your first step? Common fears that budding entrepreneurs face include:

- Fear of failure

- Fear of rejection

- Fear of not being good enough

- Surprisingly, even the fear of success

- Fear of financial risks

At first glance, these fears may seem irrational, but they are a natural part of the entrepreneurial journey. Recognizing these fears is the first step toward overcoming them. It is not about eliminating fear but learning to face it and use it as a tool for growth. Embracing your fears can offer valuable insights into your own psyche, helping you address the core issues that may be holding you back.

Fear of failure

As demonstrated by countless entrepreneurs, failure is an intrinsic part of the journey. It's not something to fear but rather something to prepare for. No one can promise guaranteed success; therefore, it's crucial to be ready for setbacks without letting them paralyze your progress.

Here are some practical ways to overcome the fear of failure:

- Set clearly defined goals

Break down your goals into manageable steps and visualize each milestone. Tools like vision boards and journals can help keep you focused and motivated.

- Address deep-seated emotions

If you have underlying anxieties, phobias, or past traumas, seek the help you need to achieve a balanced and healthy mindset. This could include therapy, meditation, or mindfulness practices. Practicing self-compassion and prioritizing your well-being is essential; don't sacrifice your happiness in pursuit of your goals.

- Rely on planning and adaptability

While uncertainty is a given in entrepreneurship, planning can provide a sense of control. Conduct risk assessments and acquire the necessary training and knowledge to build confidence. Like learning to ride a bicycle, you may fall and get bruised, but persistence is key. Keep trying until navigating the challenges becomes second nature.

- Stay adaptable

Understand that not all plans will go as expected. The more you work towards your goals, the more adaptable you become. Continuously track your progress using metrics and data to adjust your strategies as needed.

- Seek guidance and mentorship

Networking with industry leaders and mentors can provide valuable insights and support during uncertain times. Their experience can guide you through challenges more confidently.

- Avoid perfectionism

While planning is important, don't get stuck in the planning phase. The pursuit of perfection can delay progress. It's essential to start somewhere and learn from the process. Take small but steady steps towards your goals.

Fear of Rejection

Fear of rejection often emerges when pitching your ideas to investors or making sales. It can be disheartening when others don't immediately share your vision. However, remember that it's your dream, and you don't need validation from everyone. Rejection, while painful, is not the end. Instead, view it as an opportunity to learn and improve. Gather feedback, refine your approach, and adapt to new opportunities. Each rejection can bring you closer to success when you use it as a learning experience.

Fear of not being good enough

This fear is often self-imposed. The voice telling you that you're not good enough is often your own. But remember hard work and persistence can often trump innate talent. If you feel lacking in skills, invest time in developing them. Surround yourself with mentors and peers who uplift you and provide constructive feedback. Focus on your strengths and work on your weaknesses. Remember, worrying about things beyond your control is futile. Concentrate on what you can change and improve.

Combat these fears with facts. Emotions can distort your perception, making challenges seem more scary than they are. Use evidence and data to ground yourself in reality. Stop comparing yourself to others and instead focus on building your own skills and expertise. Becoming a mentor yourself can also provide a significant confidence boost as you realize the positive impact you can have on others.

Fear of success

The fear of success is an often-overlooked but real concern, stemming from feelings of impostor syndrome. When success comes, embrace it with confidence, knowing the hard work and dedication that led you there. Tracking your progress and reflecting on your efforts can help you internalize your achievements and recognize that you truly deserve them.

Ultimately, developing the entrepreneurial spirit is about overcoming these fears and moving forward with resilience, adaptability, and a willingness to learn from every experience. This journey is not about avoiding fear but learning to dance with it, using it to fuel your growth and drive your success.

Fear of financial risks

The fear of losing money over a business venture can be debilitating, and it's a completely valid concern. Not everyone has the luxury to risk their life savings or the mental resilience to start over from scratch after a financial setback. Thus, managing your financial risks is essential to alleviate such fears and build confidence in your entrepreneurial journey.

Here are some practical strategies to help you cope with the fear of financial risks:

- Prepare a strong foundation before heavy investments

Before diving into substantial investments, ensure you have a solid groundwork. This includes:

- Conducting extensive market research to understand both short-term and long-term trends and customer needs.

- Clearly define your target audience and validate your business concept with a proof of concept or minimum viable product (MVP).

- Using these insights to build a robust business plan that outlines clear goals and a strategy for achieving them.

- Start small and scale gradually

One way to mitigate financial uncertainty is to maintain your regular job while gradually building your business as a side hustle. This approach allows you to:

- Test your business model with minimal financial risk.

- Make incremental investments based on the returns and insights gained rather than committing all your resources upfront.

- Utilize outsourcing and cost-effective resources

Instead of doing everything yourself, leverage external resources to reduce costs:

- Outsource tasks that are not your core competency to freelancers or agencies, often available at competitive rates.

- Use affordable or free automation tools for repetitive tasks, allowing you to focus on strategic areas of your business.

- Explore diverse funding options

Reducing your financial burden through external funding can significantly lower your risk. Consider the following options:

- Seek out investors, venture capitalists, or crowdfunding platforms that align with your business vision.

- Look into government grants, public funding, startup incubator programs, or low-interest loans designed to support small businesses.

- Approach friends, family, or potential partners for loans or investments.

- Develop a compelling business plan and pitch to showcase your potential to prospective investors, maximizing your funding opportunities.

General Tips for Overcoming Entrepreneurial Fears

Regardless of the specific fear you're facing, the fundamental approach to overcoming any fear starts with understanding and acknowledging it.

Here are some steps to help you deal with various fears:

- Identify and acknowledge your fears

Start by identifying the fears you have and the specific concerns that trigger them. Write them down to confront them more directly, making the process of addressing them more manageable.

- Examine the basis of your fears

Analyze whether your fears are based on tangible facts or assumptions. Are they stemming from previous experiences or simply rooted in "what-ifs"? Understanding the underlying causes can help you address these fears more effectively.

- Challenge your fears through exposure

Facing your fears head-on can often diminish their power. Take inspiration from entrepreneurs like Alex Turnbull, who overcame his fear of public speaking by deliberately exposing himself to speaking opportunities. Start with smaller, less intimidating situations, and gradually increase your exposure as you build confidence.

- Seek support and learn from others

Learn from others who have successfully overcome similar fears. Join peer communities or find mentors who can offer guidance and share their experiences. Books like Do It Scared by Ruth Soukup provide practical advice and strategies for facing fears, especially those common among entrepreneurs.

- Replace negative self-talk with positive affirmations

Reframe your mindset by replacing negative self-talk with positive affirmations and self-compassion. Encourage yourself the way you would support a friend, focusing on your strengths and potential rather than your fears.

- Celebrate your achievements

No matter how small your progress, take time to celebrate your accomplishments. Recognize each step forward as a victory, boosting your motivation and reinforcing your confidence.

- Seek constructive feedback

Gain feedback from mentors, peers, and even competitors. Sometimes, an external perspective can help you see beyond your immediate fears and focus on the bigger picture. Use this feedback to refine your approach and grow your business.

- Prioritize your well-being

Your mental and physical health is crucial to your success. Practice self-care, maintain a healthy lifestyle, and ensure you have the energy and resilience needed to face challenges and fears head-on.

By understanding and addressing your fears with practical steps, you can develop the courage and resilience necessary to succeed in your entrepreneurial journey. Remember, every successful entrepreneur starts with fears and uncertainties, but what sets them apart is their willingness to confront those fears and keep moving forward.

When handling the fear of uncertainty and rejection, conducting thorough risk assessments and building solid business plans are crucial steps. These activities not only help manage fears but also play an essential role in establishing a robust foundation for your business.

Understanding Risk Assessment

Risk assessment is part of a broader process called risk analysis, which involves analyzing various aspects of a task, identifying potential threats and obstacles, prioritizing them, and devising strategies to mitigate them. It is a key decision-making tool that every business person should employ to make informed choices rather than relying solely on gut feelings. The data derived from risk assessments can provide valuable insights to support your decisions, even for the boldest of business ideas.

It's important to note that a risk assessment should not become a perfectionist exercise that hinders progress. Every task has its purpose and scope, and being overly fixated on perfecting one aspect can impede overall progress. The goal is to do your best with the resources at hand and then move on to the next steps based on the outcomes you achieve.

When to perform a risk assessment

Risk assessments should be conducted:

- At the start of any new project or when setting new goals and requirements

- When introducing changes to existing processes or systems

- Periodically, to revisit and update risk parameters, ensuring no potential hazard is overlooked

Risk assessments are also a critical part of the auditing process that businesses undergo, helping them stay compliant with regulations and improve operational safety and efficiency. For example, OSHA (Occupational Safety and Health Administration) recommends workplace risk assessments to ensure a safe environment and legal compliance.

Types of risk assessments

Risk assessments can vary in scope and scale depending on the specific needs of your business. Common types include:

- Generic risk assessment: Broad assessments applicable to multiple situations or environments, often used for initial evaluations.

- Large-scale risk assessment: Comprehensive evaluations that cover a wide range of potential risks across various departments or large projects.

- focused risk assessment: Detailed assessments targeting particular aspects of a business, such as specific processes or potential hazards.

Some examples of risk assessments commonly carried out are:

- Health and safety risk assessment: Identifies hazards that could impact the health and safety of employees or customers.

- Workplace risk assessment: Evaluates risks associated with the work environment, such as equipment hazards or ergonomic issues.

- Fall risk assessment: Focuses on preventing falls, particularly in industries like construction or manufacturing.

- Construction risk assessment: Identifies risks specific to construction sites, including structural safety and equipment hazards.

Key considerations for developing risk assessment procedures

While there are no strict rules for crafting the perfect risk assessment plan, here are some general pointers to keep in mind:

- Tailor the assessment to your business needs: Understand the unique risks associated with your business's operations and environment. Your risk assessment should be specific to these needs.

- Involve a range of stakeholders: Engage employees, management, and external experts as needed to get a comprehensive view of potential risks.

- Regularly update and review: Risks can evolve, so it's important to revisit and revise your risk assessments periodically.

- Prioritize risks based on impact and likelihood: Focus on the risks that pose the greatest threat to your business, balancing both the potential impact and the likelihood of occurrence.

- Document everything: Keep detailed records of all risk assessments, findings, and actions taken. This documentation will be valuable for audits and future reference.

- Use risk assessments to drive continuous improvement: Treat risk assessment as a cyclical process. Use the insights gained to improve existing processes and develop new strategies, fostering a culture of continuous improvement.

By following these steps and principles, you can create an effective risk assessment strategy that not only manages potential risks but also supports the growth and resilience of your business.

Mastering Business Plans: Building Confidence and Clarity

Creating a solid business plan can significantly boost your confidence when pitching your business and help eliminate doubts during execution. As I talked about business plans in my last book, The Business Plant Shortcut, a well-crafted business plan not only serves as a roadmap for your business but also as a compelling tool to attract investors, partners, and customers.

Key components of a traditional business plan

A traditional business plan typically consists of the following sections (you might want to refer to the last book for more):

- Executive summary: A brief overview of your business, its mission, and objectives.

- Company description: Detailed information about your business, including its history, structure, and what makes it unique.

- Market analysis: Insights into your industry, market size, target audience, and competitive landscape.

- Organization and management: Information about your business's organizational structure and the team behind it.

- Service or product line: A description of the products or services you offer or plan to offer.

- Marketing and sales strategy: Your plans for reaching and attracting customers, including pricing, advertising, and sales tactics.

- Funding request: If you are seeking funding, details on how much you need, why you need it, and how you plan to use it.

- Financial projections: Financial forecasts, including income statements, cash flow statements, and balance sheets.

- Appendix: Any additional information, such as resumes, permits, or other documents that support your plan.

While these components are foundational, you can tailor your business plan based on your specific needs and audience. For example, a plan for a crowdfunding campaign might be concise, while one aimed at securing a significant investment might require more detailed documentation.

Utilizing AI Tools to simplify business plan creation

Creating a comprehensive business plan can be time-consuming, but AI tools and writing software have made it easier to generate and customize plans quickly.

Here are some top AI-based business plan generators:

- Upmetrics: Offers templates and tools to help you write your business plan.

- NotionAI: Assists in organizing and drafting plans with AI-enhanced writing tools.

- Copy AI: Uses AI to generate text for different sections of your business plan.

- Grammarly: Improves the clarity and readability of your business plan.

- Beautiful AI: Creates visually appealing presentations for your business plan.

- 15MinutePlan: Enables quick, effective business plan creation with step-by-step guidance.

- WriteCream: Uses AI to help you write persuasive and engaging content.

- ProAI: Offers AI-based tools for creating comprehensive business plans.

- ChatGPT: Provides AI-generated text and insights for your business plan.

- CookUp AI: Helps in drafting business plans with easy-to-use templates.

- WordKraft AI: Assists with writing and editing business content.

- Brixx Plan Software: Offers planning tools tailored for financial forecasting.

These tools can help streamline the process of creating a business plan by providing templates, suggestions, and automated content generation. You can also refer to resources like the simple business plan template from Smartsheet to get started.

Setting goals and leveraging technology for market analysis

- Visualizing success through clear goals

To achieve your business dreams, it's essential to set clear, well-defined goals. These goals act as a compass, guiding you toward your vision and providing a framework to overcome fears and uncertainties.

- SMART Goals

A proven method to define your goals is to set SMART goals, which are:

- Specific: Clearly define what you want to achieve.

- Measurable: Establish criteria to measure your progress.

- Achievable: Ensure your goals are realistic and attainable.

- Relevant: Align your goals with your business objectives.

- Time-Bound: Set a deadline to achieve your goals.

Breaking down larger goals into smaller, actionable steps can help you focus on the immediate tasks while keeping the bigger picture in mind. This approach makes even the most ambitious dreams seem more achievable.

- Using data to strengthen goals

Data is critical in setting realistic and effective goals. It helps you determine if a goal is achievable within a specific timeframe and provides insights into market conditions and customer behaviors. To set SMART goals, gather as much relevant data as possible using a variety of analytical tools and resources.

Here are some valuable tools and platforms for conducting market research and gathering data:

- Glimpse: Provides trends and insights on emerging topics.

- Statista: Offers statistics and studies from over 600 industries.

- Think With Google Research Tools: Provides data and insights from Google's vast data network.

- Census Bureau: Offers demographic and economic data.

- Make My Persona: Helps create detailed buyer personas.

- Tableau: A data visualization tool that helps interpret complex data.

- Paperform: Allows you to create forms and surveys to collect customer insights.

- GWI: Provides global audience insights and trends.

- SurveyMonkey: An easy-to-use tool for creating surveys and collecting feedback.

- Typeform: Creates interactive surveys and forms.

- Upwave Instant Insights: Provides real-time data and insights for marketing strategies.

- Claritas MyBestSegment: Offers consumer segmentation data.

- Loop11: Conducts usability testing and gathers user feedback.

- Userlytics: Provides user testing and feedback services.

- Temper: Gathers user sentiment and feedback.

- NielsenIQ: Provides consumer data and analytics.

- Ubersuggest: A keyword research tool that also offers SEO insights.

- Pew Research Center: Offers reports on public opinion and demographic research.

- BrandMentions: Monitors brand mentions and tracks competitors.

- Qualtrics Market Research Panels: Provides access to a broad range of market research data.

- Qualaroo: Collects user insights directly on your website.

By using these tools, you can gather the data needed to set SMART goals, refine your business strategy, and enhance your understanding of market dynamics.

With a solid business plan and clear, data-driven goals, you will be better equipped to navigate the challenges of building your business and turn your vision into reality.

Wrap Up

In this chapter, we explored the importance of the entrepreneurial mindset, its resilience, and how it shapes an entrepreneur's journey. You learned about developing an unbreakable spirit, recognizing and facing fears, and using failures as stepping stones toward success.

Action Steps

1. Reflect on your personal fears about starting a business and write them down.

2. Set specific goals that can help you manage and reduce these fears.

3. Find a mentor or join a community of entrepreneurs for support and guidance.

Up Next

In the next chapter, we'll explore the foundational elements of building a business. You'll learn about choosing the right structure, staying legally compliant, and setting up strong financial systems—ensuring your business is grounded on a solid foundation.

Chapter Two

Building a Strong Foundation

There are multiple reasons why businesses succeed (or fail, for that matter). But the common theme among successful ventures is they enjoy a strong foundation. This strong foundation enables them to withstand market-driven earthquakes and self-inflicted tsunamis (hiring error, incorrect budget allocation, etc).

Thus, the next step to building a business is constructing a strong foundation.

What does it look like? Among other things, a strong foundation is financially sound and legally compliant. At the end of the day, no business can exist without capital. Furthermore, no business can survive by upsetting the regulators.

Take the case of Enron. In the early 2000s, the energy company became synonymous with corporate fraud after it was revealed that its executives had engaged in accounting fraud and deceptive business practices. More specifically, Enron created a network of SPEs to offload debt and liabilities from its balance sheet, making the company appear more financially stable than it actually was. The scandal led to the company's bankruptcy and the imprisonment of several of its executives.

To prevent such threatening scenarios, you must always keep your business in compliance. And it requires you to choose the right business structure.

If you've never dealt with structuring a business before or are familiar with finance, relax; it's not the end of the world. It doesn't mean you should throw in the towel.

In this chapter, we delve deeper into the types of business structures and help you pick the right one. Along with that, we'll learn about the key jargon used in the legal world. Then, we'll go through the basic concepts in accounting and finance that'll help you keep your business financially sound.

By the end of the chapter, you will have the knowledge to work with local regulators, audit your business, and handle finances on your own.

The Basics of Business Structures

Selecting the appropriate business structure is a foundational decision for any aspiring entrepreneur. This choice can significantly impact your business's legal, financial, and operational aspects. The structure you choose determines your legal liability, tax obligations, and how your business is governed.

A well-informed decision can provide a solid foundation for your venture, while a misstep could lead to unnecessary complications and challenges.

Liability: Your Personal Risk Exposure

Arguably, the main reason why nailing down the right business structure is important is because of liability.

Liability in business refers to the legal responsibility of a business entity or its owners for debts, obligations, and legal actions. This can include damages, fines, or other financial penalties. For example, if a business or its employees engage in negligent or harmful behavior, the business may be liable for any resulting damages. Different business structures offer varying levels of liability protection.

Taxes: How Much You Owe to the State

All businesses pay taxes, but not every business is taxed in the same way. How your business will be taxed will depend on the business structure. The tax rates for individuals and corporations vary, and your choice of structure can affect your overall tax burden.

Moreover, Different structures may offer different opportunities for deductions and credits, which can reduce your tax liability.

Capital: The Ease With Which You Can Access It

Capital is the lifeblood of a business. Especially when starting a business, you need to have access to capital until you hit breakeven. This is also crucial during distressful times like the recent COVID-19 pandemic lockdowns.

The type of business structure you choose can significantly impact your ability to obtain financing. By understanding the factors that influence capital access and developing a strong business plan, you can improve your chances of securing the necessary financing for your venture.

Succession Planning: What Will Happen When You Move on

Nearly 45% of the businesses fail within five years. But the 55% that make it through need to have succession planning in place. This succession plan legally formulates what will happen to the business once the founder decides to hang up his/her boots. It involves creating a plan for transferring ownership and management responsibilities to future generations or external parties.

And the transition complexity depends on how the business is structured. A well-executed succession plan ensures that the business can continue to operate smoothly even after the founders' departure.

4 Types of Business Structure

As you proceed to register your business, you'll have to specify a structure. In the United States, for-profit businesses usually fall into four categories. These are:

- Sole Proprietorship

- Partnership

- LLC or Limited Liability Company

- Corporation

Let's explore each category in more detail.

Sole Proprietorship

The most basic structure that's easy to set up and manage is sole proprietorship. As a self-explanatory phrase, it's a business owned and operated by a single individual. There may be a few employees or contractors, but it's usually the owner doing all the heavy lifting. This structure is often suitable for small, home-based businesses or those just starting out.

Here are the key characteristics of a sole proprietorship business:

- Single and complete ownership – The owner has complete ownership of the business and is the sole operator of the business.

- No formal structure – As there are no stakeholders, there's no structure or hierarchy with which a sole proprietorship operates.

- Unlimited personal liability – There is no legal separation between the business and the owner, making him/her personally responsible for the business's actions. This means their personal assets, such as their home and savings, can be at risk.

- Pass-through taxation - Profits and losses from a sole proprietorship are reported on the owner's personal income tax return. This is known as pass-through taxation, which eliminates double taxation.

- No separate legal entity – Lastly, understand that a sole proprietorship is not a separate legal entity from the owner. The business is considered an extension of the owner.

So, is sole proprietorship a good idea? There are pros and cons to it.

Pros

- Easy to set up

- Complete control of the business

- Flexibility with operations

Cons

- No liability protection, leaving the owner vulnerable to lawsuits and penalties

- Limited access to capital

- Succession planning can be complicated

Partnership

A partnership is a business structure where two or more individuals share ownership and responsibilities. This is an upgrade from a sole proprietorship business with added complexities and hurdles.

Partnerships are common when the founders come with different skills, have a shared vision, and are willing to work as partners. They forge a partnership and the profits and losses are shared among the partners according to their partnership agreement. This can be based on equal shares, agreed-upon percentages, or other factors.

There are two main types of partnerships: general partnerships and limited partnerships. Here's how they differ:

General partnership

- Shared ownership – The partners are co-owners of the business, with equal rights and responsibilities unless otherwise specified in the partnership agreement.

- Unlimited liability – Each general partner is personally liable for all of the partnership's financial obligations, including those caused by the negligence or misconduct of other partners.

- Shared profits and losses – Both the profits and losses are shared by the partners based on the predetermined agreement.

- Joint management – In a general partnership, all partners have an equal say in the management of the business unless otherwise specified. This means that major decisions require consensus among the partners.

<u>Limited partnership</u>

- Limited and general partners – A limited partnership has at least one general partner with unlimited liability and one or more limited partners with limited liability.

- Limited liability – Limited partners are only responsible for the amount they originally invested and are not personally liable for the partnership's debts. However, they do not have a say in the management of the business.

- Limited involvement – Limited partners typically have limited involvement in the management of the business. Their role is primarily to invest capital in the partnership and share in the profits.

- Profit sharing – Limited partners share in the profits of the partnership but are not liable for its losses beyond their initial investment.

So, is partnership a good idea? Here are the pros and cons of this structure

Pros

- Shared resources and expertise

- Increased capital and funding

- Support network due to the involvement of more partners

Cons

- Higher failure rate due to conflict of interest

- Unlimited liability for general partners

LLC

The Small Business Administration (SBA) reports that LLCs are the most popular business structure for new businesses formed in the US. There are several reasons why new entrepreneurs opt for an LLC or Limited Liability Company over others. But know that it's a hybrid business structure that combines elements of a corporation (the last structure type) and a partnership. It offers the limited liability protection of a corporation while maintaining the pass-through taxation of a partnership or sole proprietorship.

Here are the key characteristics of an LLC business:

- Limited liability - LLC members are not personally liable for the company's obligations. This means their personal assets are generally protected. As an LLC is a separate legal entity from its members, it provides a layer of protection.

- Pass-through taxation – By default, LLCs are taxed as pass-through entities.

- Flexible management structure - LLCs offer flexibility in terms of management. They can be member-managed, where all members are involved in management, or manager-managed, where designated managers oversee the business.

- Operating agreement - An LLC is governed by an operating agreement, a legal document that outlines the rights, responsibilities, and ownership interests of the members. This document is used to settle disputes arising among the members.

- Perpetual life - LLCs can have perpetual life, meaning they can continue to exist even if members change. This provides stability and continuity for the business.

So why choose LLC over others? Here are the pros (followed by cons):

Pros

- Liability protection

- LLCs are perceived as more credible

- Better succession planning

Cons

- Potential for double taxation

- More reporting to regulators

- Ownership transfer restrictions

Corporation

The biggest and most complex business structure is a corporation. Corporations are a suitable business structure for larger businesses with a higher scale of operation and more shareholders. While the specific requirements can vary by jurisdiction, corporations generally involve more paperwork, legal formalities, and ongoing compliance obligations compared to sole proprietorships or partnerships.

Here are the key characteristics of corporations:

- Separate legal entity - A corporation is a distinct legal entity and it can sue, be sued, enter into contracts, and own property in its own name.

- Limited liability – The corporation structure provides liability protection to its owners. Thus, their personal assets are protected, even if the corporation faces financial difficulties or legal claims.

- Double taxation - Corporations face double taxation. This means the corporation pays corporate income tax on its profits, and shareholders pay personal income tax on dividends they receive.

- Management structure - Corporations typically have a board of directors and management team that oversee the business's operations.

- Stringent regulatory compliance - Corporations are subject to various regulatory requirements, including filing financial statements and complying with securities laws.

Here are the pros and cons of Corporations:

Pros

- Better access to capital

- Limited liability

- Can operate at a bigger scale

Cons

- Expensive to set up and maintain

- Double taxation

- Subject to heavy scrutiny

Picking the right structure for your business is crucial. Therefore, spend a fair amount of time deciding on which structure to opt for your venture.

Setting Up a Business Structure

Once you've determined the ideal structure, time to navigate the legal maze and register the business. Previously, setting up a business was a challenging and expensive affair. But thanks to technology, it's now much simpler. Here are the steps involved in setting up a business:

- Pick and register a business name

Choosing your business name is like picking your identity, and it's a legal requirement to get it registered. If you're going to operate under a name different from your LLC or Corporation, you'll need to file for a DBA (Doing Business As).

Before you fall in love with a name, make sure it's available! You can search your state's business registry or the US Patent and Trademark Office (USPTO) database. With over 33 million small businesses in the US, competition for good names is fierce.

- Trademark your assets

Getting a name isn't enough. You need to trademark it along with other assets like slogans and logos. This ensures others can't copy or misuse your assets.

File with the USPTO. The US Patent and Trademark Office handles this. The process can take a few months, but it's worth it. Think of it as insurance for your brand's reputation.

- Apply for Federal Tax ID number (EIN)

Just like a social security number for individuals, your business needs a unique identifier—an Employer Identification Number (EIN). It's required if you plan on hiring employees or forming a corporation.

You can get it online directly from the IRS. With your EIN, you'll be set to file taxes, open a business bank account, and apply for any necessary licenses.

- Open a business bank account

Once you have the EIN number, you should open a business bank account. Separating personal and business finances isn't just good practice—it's the law if you have an LLC or Corporation. A business account helps you track your revenue, manage expenses, and look more professional. Plus, you may receive credit and loan offers from banks with a bank account!

- Determine if you need a state tax ID number

On top of your federal EIN, many states require businesses to get a State Tax ID—especially if you'll be paying state taxes like income or sales tax. Rules vary, so check with your state's Department of Revenue. For example, in states like California, you'll need this ID for any sales tax reporting.

- Obtain permits and licenses

Depending on your industry and location, you might need special licenses to operate. For example, food services, construction, and other regulated industries require permits. Skipping this step could lead to hefty fines or even shutdowns.

- Get business insurance

Nearly 60% of businesses are sued annually. Thus, business insurance is non-negotiable. It's there to protect you from the unexpected—whether it's a lawsuit, an accident or a natural disaster.

There are different types of insurance, but general liability insurance is the most common. It provides the best level of protection for your business. Also, you should consider workers' compensation insurance (if you have employees) and professional liability insurance (if you offer services).

- Hire and classify employees

Unless you're a sole proprietor and a one-man army, you need to hire. This involves posting ads, screening candidates, interviewing them, and offering a job offer. Or you can work with employment agencies to handle it for you.

But the next step to hiring is classifying. Note that 30% of companies incorrectly classify employees, leading to back taxes and penalties. Employees get tax withholdings and benefits, while contractors don't. Be clear on the difference!

- Comply with labor laws

Labor laws are in place to protect both you and your employees. These laws cover everything from minimum wage to workplace safety standards. Thus, familiarize yourself with the Fair Labor Standards Act (FLSA) and Occupational Safety and Health Administration (OSHA) regulations and make sure you comply.

- Keep good records

Good record-keeping is crucial for staying on top of taxes, tracking financial health, and avoiding compliance issues. You'll need to maintain clear records of income, expenses, payroll, and tax documents. Invest in an accounting system—whether it's QuickBooks, Xero, or even an Excel spreadsheet.

- Consult the professionals

At the end of the day, professional help goes a long way. Starting a business involves many legal and financial complexities. From taxes to contracts, working with professionals can save you headaches and money. Thus, consult with a lawyer, accountant or business advisor and seek specialist help in areas where you're falling short.

Basics of Accounting, Bookkeeping, and Financial Management

Based on the data, I know most of you don't have a bookkeeping background. Bookkeeping might sound like a complicated world full of jargon, but once you break it down, it's not so bad. And from a finance standpoint, it is super important.

Below, I'll explain some of the most important terms in bookkeeping using everyday examples so you can feel confident handling your business's finances.

- Assets

Think of assets as everything your business owns that has value. It could be cash, equipment, buildings, or even the computer you're reading this on. Assets are like the tools in your toolbox—they help you run and grow your business.

For example, if you own a bakery, your assets would include your oven, the cash in your bank account, and any supplies like flour and sugar.

- Liabilities

Liabilities are the opposite of assets—they're what your business owes to others. This could be money you owe suppliers, loans you've taken out, or bills you haven't paid yet. Think of liabilities as your financial "to-do" list.

For example, if you borrowed $10,000 to buy that bakery oven, that loan is a liability.

- Equity

Equity is what's left over after you subtract your liabilities from your assets. In other words, it's the portion of the business that belongs to you (or the owners). Imagine it as the slice of the pie that's yours after everyone else gets paid.

For example, if your bakery has $50,000 in assets and $20,000 in liabilities, your equity is $30,000. That's the value of your business that you own outright.

- Single-Entry Bookkeeping

Single-entry bookkeeping is the simpler method of tracking your finances. You record transactions like income and expenses once. It's like keeping a checkbook, where you jot down how much you make and how much you spend.

like a savings account for your business—it's money that stays in the business to help it grow.

For example if your bakery made $5,000 in profit last year, but instead of taking all of it as income, you left $2,000 in the business, that $2,000 is your retained earnings.

Setting up Accounting System

Bookkeeping goes hand in hand with accounting. While the former is about recording the transactions, accounting is analyzing, summarizing, and reporting the data.

Again, this may seem complicated. But once you're aware of the entire process, things become much more manageable. Here are the steps involved in accounting:

- Itemize All Expenses by Department

As your business grows, your expenses will grow, too. To keep things clear, start by itemizing expenses by category or department. This could be marketing, operations, inventory, or payroll. Doing this helps you see exactly where your money is going and if any department is overspending.

- Adhere to all income, employment, and excise taxes

Reporting on taxes is the fundamental duty of accounting. Depending on your business type, you'll need to stay on top of income taxes, employment taxes (if you have employees), and possibly excise taxes (for specific goods like alcohol, tobacco, or gasoline).

You'll need to report your business income to the IRS. If you're a sole proprietor, you'll report this on your personal tax return. For corporations or LLCs, it gets a little more complicated, so a CPA might help.

- Set up a payroll system

If you're hiring employees, one of the first things you need is a solid payroll system. This system should calculate employee wages, withhold the right taxes, and issue payments on time.

- Double-Entry Bookkeeping

Double-entry bookkeeping is a more accurate method where every transaction is recorded twice: once as a "debit" and once as a "credit." This ensures that your books are always balanced (think of it like balancing scales).

- Cash Basis of Accounting

The cash basis of accounting is a simple method where you record income when you actually receive cash and expenses when you pay them. It's like tracking the money as it moves in and out of your wallet.

For example, if you sell a cake today and the customer pays you $100, you record that $100 now. If you pay for ingredients tomorrow, you record that payment tomorrow.

- Accrual Basis of Accounting

The accrual basis of accounting records income and expenses when they happen, not when the money changes hands. It's like marking a check on your calendar the day you send it, even if it hasn't been cashed yet.

For example, if you deliver a cake today but won't get paid until next week, you still record the income today. Same for expenses—if you bought ingredients today but haven't paid for them yet, you record the expense now.

- Income Statement

An income statement (sometimes called a profit and loss statement) is like a report card for your business. It shows your income, expenses, and whether you made a profit or suffered a loss over a specific period.

At the end of the month, your bakery's income statement might show $10,000 in sales and $7,000 in expenses, leaving you with $3,000 in profit.

- Retained Earnings

Retained earnings are the profits your business has made over time that you've decided to keep rather than pay out to yourself or other owners. Think of retained earnings

Invest in payroll software that automates calculations, tax withholdings, and even direct deposit, freeing up your time to focus on growing the business.

- Identify the right payment gateway

If you're handling online sales, choosing the right payment gateway is essential. A payment gateway is a service that processes credit card payments for e-commerce. Think of it as the virtual cash register for your online store. PayPal, Stripe, and Square are some popular payment gateways that make it easy to process payments from customers around the world.

Most payment gateways integrate seamlessly with accounting software, making reporting more accurate.

Some gateways are better for small businesses, while others are designed for higher-volume transactions. So do some homework.

- Regularly review and evaluate your processes

No accounting system is "set it and forget it." Regularly reviewing your processes and financial reports helps you stay on top of your finances. Evaluate whether your current methods are working or if you need to upgrade software, adjust budgeting categories, or hire help.

- Consult with a professional or CPA

Last but not least, don't hesitate to bring in the pros. Consulting a CPA (Certified Public Accountant) or a financial advisor can save you money in the long run. They can help you with taxes, make sure your accounting system is compliant, and even offer advice on scaling your business.

Wrap Up

This chapter walked you through building a strong foundation for your business, from picking the right structure to navigating legal and financial essentials. With these basics in place, you're setting yourself up for stability and success as you start your journey.

Action Steps

1. Decide which business structure best aligns with your goals.

2. Register your business and obtain any permits or licenses needed.

3. Set up a simple accounting system to track finances from day one.

Up Next

Now that you've set the foundation, it's time to get ready for the big launch! In the next chapter, we'll cover the final steps before going live, from creating your workspace to organizing your operations so you can hit the ground running.

Chapter Three

Launching with Confidence

As your business's launch date nears, you may experience sleepless nights. Staying awake late brooding about the perfect marketing slogan or ideal workstation can be stressful and unproductive.

To get out of this overthinking maze, you need to set your ducks in the row for the launch. This involves creating an infrastructure where you can deliver the products and services to the customers. In other words, you need to set up an office and/or workshop.

When many of us dream of starting a business, we envision the ideal setup: the perfect logo, a beautiful website, and a workspace that makes us feel like real entrepreneurs. But it's a huge trap—one I've fallen into myself, spending far too long on aesthetics instead of just getting started. The reality is, some of the world's biggest companies began with minimal resources. Amazon, for example, famously used desks made from doors to save money, even when they were successful enough to afford more. Large companies like Google and Apple started in garages with basic setups, focusing on testing their ideas rather than perfecting every detail upfront.

Starting lean with a minimum viable product (MVP) allows you to test your idea without a major upfront investment. If you're starting an internet business, you can even keep your day job, working on your idea during evenings and weekends. This "lean" approach lets you focus on making the business self-sustaining before you go all in. Avoiding the setup trap means keeping your focus where it counts—on growth, customers, and real progress. I've made these mistakes myself, and I'm here to help you avoid learning it the hard way!

Building an office doesn't necessarily mean renting a space in the upmarket commercial area. This would drive up the cost by hundreds of thousands of dollars. In fact, in this digital age, you don't even need a physical space if your niche permits. You can set up a virtual store and deliver from the comfort of your home. These home-based businesses are both easy to set up and cost-effective.

For this, you need to get technology on your side and leverage it to the fullest. And that's what this chapter is about – giving you all the technical details to launch your business with confidence.

This chapter is divided into three key sections: setting up a home-based business, setting up a brick-and-mortar business, and launching an online business.

Also, you'll learn the latest tricks and tactics to leverage AI to further your business goals. Rest assured, everything is explained in layman's terms with limited technical jargon. So, you won't need a diploma in computer science to go through this chapter.

A Home-Based Business

In this inflated economy with rising cost rental costs, businesses are on the lookout to cut costs. One way the smart money managers are doing it is by cutting their dependence on office space. Office space is no longer a prerequisite to launching a business.

In fact, the home-based business model has become increasingly popular, offering entrepreneurs the freedom and flexibility to operate from the comfort of their own space.

The US Small Business Association reports that50% of all small businesses begin at home. In fact, tech giants like Apple and Google also started at home. In 1998, Larry Page and Sergey Brin, then graduate students at Stanford University, founded Google in their garage.

The single biggest benefit to starting a home-based business is reduced upfront capital. You don't have to set aside money for office rent or maintenance, nor have to lock yourself into extended contracts.

However, there are a few things you need to know before you launch a home-based business.

Zoning Laws

All land in the United States falls under zoning laws. These laws determine what types of activities are permitted in different zones, such as residential, commercial, or industrial.

Some areas may have restrictions on home-based businesses, particularly those that involve significant customer traffic or noise.

For example, in a residential zone, you might be allowed to operate a small office-based business but prohibited from running a large-scale or mid-scale manufacturing facility.

Note that zoning laws are local-specific. Thus, it's important to check with your city or county's zoning department to ensure your business activity complies with local regulations.

License and Permits

In most cases, you will need a business license from your city or county to legally operate, even if the business is home-based.

Depending on the niche of your home-based business, you may need to obtain specific licenses or permits from your local government. These can include:

- Business license: A general license required for operating a business within a jurisdiction.

- Home occupation permit: A specific permit that allows you to conduct business activities from your home.

- Professional licenses: If you're providing professional services (e.g., legal, medical, accounting), you may need to have a professional license.

- Sales tax license: If your business involves selling products, you may need a state sales tax permit.

Ensure you have all the permits in place before you launch.

HOA (Homeowners Association) Rules

It's highly unlikely you're alone in the middle of a wilderness. Chances are you're living in a society. And if you're living in a community governed by an HOA, their rules may have restrictions on home-based businesses.

HOAs often specify if commercial operations are permitted within the community. And if so, they may have restrictions on:

- Number of employees - HOA may limit the number of employees working from home.

- Customer traffic - HOA might restrict the amount of customer traffic to and from your home.

- Business hours - It may specify the hours during which you can operate your business.

- Noise levels - HOA may have noise restrictions to prevent disturbances to neighbors.

So, check with the rules and ensure you're not breaching any of them.

Insurance

It's important to review your homeowner's insurance policy to ensure it covers potential business-related liabilities. You may need to purchase additional coverage to protect your assets and business operations.

If a client gets injured on your property while conducting business, your homeowner's insurance may or may not cover the liability.

Mortgage or Lease Impact

If you're renting or have a mortgage on your home, you should check your lease or mortgage agreement for any restrictions on home-based businesses.

For example, your lease might prohibit you from operating a business that involves heavy machinery or frequent deliveries. Alternatively, you might need to provide notice to your landlord or lender before starting a home-based business.

So, unless it is a property you own, you need to get on the same page with your landlord or mortgage provider.

A Brick-and-Mortar Business

There are times when setting up a home business is not an option. For example, perhaps the HOA does not permit you to set up a shop. Or your customers are unwilling to travel the distance to your home.

In such cases, your next best (and cost-effective) option is to set up a brick-and-mortar business. A brick-and-mortar business is a traditional business that has a physical storefront or location. These businesses are the soul of the American entrepreneurial spirit and dominate the business landscape.

Some examples of these storefronts include grocery stores, restaurants, salons, gyms, pet shops, etc.

Starting a brick-and-mortar business involves more complexity and regulatory oversight compared to a home-based business. This is primarily due to the use of a physical commercial space, which brings additional legal, zoning, and operational requirements.

In addition to the permits required for home-based businesses, you will have to apply for some more. And this depends on the location you're in.

But in general, you'll have to take care of the following:

Building Permits

Brick-and-mortar businesses need a commercial location to operate. These locations must be in line with the local regulations. Whether you are building new or renovating, building permits ensure that your construction adheres to local building codes, zoning regulations, and safety standards.

Authorities will conduct inspections to determine suitability and verify compliance. Moreover, the fire department will inspect the premises to ensure they meet fire safety standards, including having the appropriate fire exits, alarms, and fire extinguishing systems. If you operate in industries like food service, healthcare, or personal care (e.g., hair salons), you'll need to pass a health inspection to ensure sanitary conditions and safe operations.

After inspection, you'll get the license and clearance needed to launch your brick-and-mortar business.

EIN

We've already touched on EIN or Employer Identification Number in the previous chapter. But it's worth reiterating here.

An EIN is a nine-digit number assigned by the IRS to US businesses for tax purposes. If you plan to hire employees, you'll need an EIN to report and pay employment taxes. Even sole proprietors often obtain an EIN to keep their Social Security Number private.

Thus, apply for and obtain an EIN. If you're residing outside the U.S., I recommend reviewing your country's tax laws and taking appropriate action based on them.

You can take ChatGPT's help using this prompt:

Can you help me find the tax laws in [Country/Region]? I'm looking for information on [specific tax topic, e.g., income tax, corporate tax, tax filing requirements, etc.] for businesses in [Country/Region].

Alternatively, asking your tax-law attorney or certified public accountant is highly recommended

Sales Tax Permit

As a brick-and-mortar business, you're generally responsible for collecting sales tax from your customers and remitting it to the appropriate tax authority.

You'll need to calculate the sales tax amount based on the purchase price and the applicable tax rate. The tax is typically collected from the customer at the time of sale and included in the total purchase price.

However, some goods and services may be exempt from sales tax, such as essential items, charitable donations, or certain types of business-to-business transactions. It's better if you familiarize yourself with the sales tax exemptions in your jurisdiction.

Here's a prompt you can use to ask for help with sales tax collection:

Can you guide me through the process of collecting and remitting sales tax for my brick-and-mortar business? I need help understanding:

- How to calculate the sales tax based on the purchase price and applicable tax rate

- When and how to collect the tax from customers during a sale

- How to remit the collected sales tax to the correct tax authority

After collection, you'll have to file sales tax returns periodically. The frequency will depend on your state's requirements and the amount of sales tax collected. You'll also need to remit the collected sales tax to the tax authority within the specified deadline.

Signage And Adverts Permit

Most municipalities regulate the types of signs businesses can display on the exterior of the building. Brick-and-mortar businesses must navigate these regulations carefully to avoid penalties or having to remove non-compliant signs.

Local regulations often specify the maximum and minimum size of signs allowed for businesses. The type of signage can also be restricted, such as illuminated signs, billboards, banners, sandwich boards, or digital displays.

There are also restrictions and specifications on placement, visibility, height, design, content, and even frequency. For example, in Stanton, California, brick-and-mortar businesses are allowed no more than six banner permits per year. Likewise, Garland, Texas, allows banners within the first 20 days of opening the store.

You can visit your local city's website for detailed information on specific permit requirements relevant to your location.

Here is a sample ChatGPT prompt:

Can you help me find the permit requirements for [specific activity or business] in [City/Region]? I'm looking for detailed information on local regulations and any necessary permits for this location.

Environmental Permit

There are certain brick-and-mortar businesses that will need an environmental permit. These permits are typically required when a business's operations involve emissions to air, land, or water, waste management, use of hazardous substances, or activities that may cause pollution.

Businesses that release pollutants into the air - manufacturing plants, auto body shops, and even large-scale dry cleaners - will need an air emission permit.

Similarly, businesses that discharge wastewater or other substances into local water bodies, such as manufacturers, food processors, and breweries, will require water discharge permits.

Developers, construction companies, and businesses that engage in activities that disturb the soil or natural habitats, such as excavation, grading, or clearing land, will have to obtain land disturbance permits.

Many environmental permits are mandated by laws such as the Clean Air Act, the Clean Water Act, and the Endangered Species Act. If you fail to obtain and comply with these permits, it may result in fines, lawsuits, and even the shutdown of the business.

Insurance

Insurance coverage is even more important if you're opening a brick-and-mortar store. It provides financial protection in the event of unexpected losses or liabilities.

The specific types of insurance needed will vary depending on the nature of your business and the risks involved. Some of the most common ones are property insurance, general liability insurance, commercial auto insurance, product liability insurance, PDO (property damage to others), and workers' compensation insurance.

Here is a sample ChatGPT prompt:

Can you help me determine the types of insurance I need for my business in [Industry/Type of Business]? I want to understand the specific coverage options, such as property insurance, liability insurance, workers' compensation, or others that are relevant to my business risks.

Labor Laws

If you're going to have employees working at your brick-and-mortar location, you'll have to comply with the local labor laws. These laws are designed to protect workers' rights and set minimum standards for employment conditions, such as wages, hours, workplace safety, and anti-discrimination practices.

Here is how you can find regional labor laws in the US:

- Reach out to your state's Department of Labor: State laws may provide additional protections beyond federal regulations.

- Contact your local OSHA office: For more information, call 1-800-321-OSHA.

- Visit the U.S. Equal Employment Opportunity Commission (EEOC) website: For further details, call 1-800-669-4000 or visit www.eeoc.gov.

The Fair Labor Standards Act (FLSA) sets federal minimum wage standards, although many states have their own higher minimum wages. Likewise, the Occupational Safety and Health Act (OSHA) enforces safety standards, requiring employers to address potential workplace risks such as machinery, hazardous chemicals, and fire hazards.

Here is a sample ChatGPT prompt:

Can you help me find the labor laws specific to [State/Region]? I'm looking for information on [specific labor law topic, e.g., minimum wage, overtime, workplace safety, employee rights, etc.] in that area.

Remember that as a business owner, it's on you to keep your employees safe and happy.

An Online Business

Now, let's discuss the third type of business and how to launch it: online ventures. These are a newer type of business that offers full flexibility to both owners and employees. An online business can be run from home, but it doesn't have to be. Some operate entirely remotely, while others may combine online operations with a physical presence, depending on the business model.

An online business operates primarily or entirely through the Internet and doesn't require a physical storefront or location. Online businesses can sell products, services, or digital content directly to customers through their websites and/or online marketplaces.

While many home-based businesses also operate online, online businesses are specifically designed to leverage the Internet as their primary platform. They may or may not have a physical location, but their core operations and customer interactions occur online.

One of the major benefits of an online business is its potential for global reach. An online business can serve customers from any part of the world, and the scalability is often easier compared to traditional or home-based businesses, as it's not limited by location. In comparison, a home-based business usually operates within a specific geographical region or local area, especially if the service requires physical presence.

Of the three, online businesses are easier to start and run. And in most cases, you won't need permits as well.

However, there are some key regulations and requirements for online businesses in the US. These are:

Business License

Nearly every business in the United States requires some type of license or permit to operate legally, with a business license being the most common..

Sales Tax

If you sell tangible goods or services to customers, you're generally required to collect and remit sales tax. Similarly, you'll have to file self-employment taxes if you're a sole proprietor or LLC. You will need to pay federal, state, and local taxes on your earnings. Make sure to track all business-related expenses, as these can be deducted from your income when filing taxes.

EIN

You'll need an Employer Identification Number from the IRS for tax purposes, even if you don't have employees.

Here is a sample ChatGPT prompt:

Can you guide me on how to obtain an Employer Identification Number (EIN) from the IRS for tax purposes, even if I don't have any employees? I need to know the process and any requirements for applying.

Consumer Protection Laws

Online businesses must comply with federal and state consumer protection laws, such as the Federal Trade Commission Act and state truth-in-advertising laws. The

FTC Act prohibits unfair or deceptive business practices, including false advertising, misleading claims, and deceptive pricing.

Here is a sample prompt through which you can take ChatGPT's help to extract more information:

Can you provide an overview of consumer protection laws in [Country/Region]? I'm particularly interested in understanding how these laws apply to [specific industry or scenario, e.g., retail, e-commerce, product warranties, false advertising, etc.], and what businesses need to do to ensure compliance.

Data Privacy Laws

Online businesses collect data regularly. Businesses that collect and store customer data must comply with data privacy laws, such as the General Data Protection Regulation (GDPR) and local-level data privacy laws.

Here is a sample prompt through which you can take ChatGPT's help to extract more information:

Can you help me understand data privacy laws in [Country/Region]? I'm looking for information on compliance requirements, particularly regarding [specific aspect, e.g., data collection, storage, sharing, or user consent], and how these laws apply to businesses handling customer data.

Building a Home Workspace

Companies invest a huge amount of money into creating the best workplace for their employees. Enough research concludes that the office setting has a direct impact on creativity, productivity, and team environment.

When you work from home, you must create an inspiring workspace. Your home workspace is more than just a place to work; it's a catalyst for success.

In this section, we'll delve into the art of creating a home workspace that inspires, motivates, and elevates your entrepreneurial journey.

Designate a dedicated workspace

When you're working from home, any corner of the house may be suitable for work. But it's best if you specify a workspace. A dedicated workspace, even if it's just a corner of a room, helps separate your business activities from your personal life. It creates a psychological distinction between "work mode" and "home mode," which improves focus and reduces distractions.

If possible, an entire room is the best option. This ensures you can work distraction-free for hours, especially if you have a family with small children. If not, you can utilize the spare space in the garage, attic, or living room.

Invest in the right furniture

Office-specific furniture will support your work for an extended period, ensuring you stay productive. If you already have the furniture, great! If not, we've got some shopping to do.

Invest in an ergonomic chair that supports your back and promotes good posture. Then, choose a desk that suits your work style (standing desks are becoming popular to promote movement). As an optional item, you can consider adding storage units and shelves.

A stable internet connectivity

The Internet will be your gateway to the outside world. It's the lifeline that connects you to your customers, suppliers, and the digital world.

Thus, invest in a fast and reliable internet connection. If available in your area, consider a fiber-optic connection or cable internet. When prospecting your options, be aware of any data limits imposed by the internet service providers (ISPs). If your business relies heavily on data usage, consider unlimited plans or plans with generous data allowances.

Having a backup internet connection, such as a mobile hotspot, can be helpful in case of outages. Therefore, also invest in proper data plans.

Ensure proper lighting

Imagine a dimly lit, shadowy workspace. Does it inspire you to get up and work? Probably not. Good lighting is more than just a necessity; it's a powerful tool that can transform your home office into a haven of productivity and inspiration.

Poor lighting can also lead to fatigue, headaches, and blurred vision. Adequate lighting helps prevent these problems and keeps you focused for longer.

Create a power backup

If you live in an area with constant power outages, you must plan for them through power backup solutions. Think of uninterrupted power supplies (UPSs) and batteries that keep your devices running even after power failure.

Determine the wattage and power requirements of your equipment to select the appropriate backup system. Also, consider how long you need your system to provide backup power during outages.

Keep office supplies handy

By maintaining a well-stocked supply closet, you can ensure that you have everything you need to stay organized and productive in your home-based office.

So, prior to launching your business, buy essential office supplies, preferably in bulk. This includes pens, pencils, paper, envelopes, glue, notebooks, binders, file folders, etc.

Getting Tech on Your Side

Many folks, especially the older generation, starting a business for the first time see tech as an overwhelming hindrance. They follow the outdated mantra of "Build it, and they'll come."

But in this digital age, tech is no longer optional. The tech-driven economy isn't kind enough to spare those not utilizing tech to the fullest. This becomes even more important as you're launching a home-based or online business where foot traffic is non-existent.

Here are the ways to get tech on your side:

Build a website

At the very least, you need a website for your business. This is your home in the digital world where your customers and clients can interact and learn more about you.

Use website builders like WordPress, Wix, or Squarespace to create a professional-looking website. These platforms offer customizable templates and easy-to-use tools for building and managing your site without needing advanced coding skills. Or you can hire a professional WordPress or Wix designer from platforms like Upwork and Fiverr to do it for you.

If you plan to sell online, consider upgrading to an e-commerce website that allows you to handle orders.

Invest in a CRM and project management tool

Along with the website, it's highly recommended that you get customer relationship management (CRM) and project management software. These are essential to managing and running your everyday business.

Implement CRM software like HubSpot, Salesforce, or Zoho CRM to manage customer interactions, track leads, and analyze sales data. These tools help streamline communication, improve customer service, and help you manage your team.

For project management, you can opt for Trello, Asana, or Monday.com. These tools help keep projects organized and ensure timely completion.

Leverage social media

With 5.07 billion people active on social media, it's important to focus on the platforms where your ideal customers spend their time. For example, if your target audience is younger, platforms like Instagram or TikTok might be key. For a professional audience, LinkedIn is a good choice, while Facebook remains popular across a range of age groups. Being present where your audience is already active lets you effectively showcase your products and services.

Being active on social media also helps you build trust, which is especially important when you're new. In a HubSpot survey, 49% confessed to trusting brands that sell directly on social media platforms.

While the list is long, you should choose the platforms that are best for your niche. Instagram is particularly suited for the food, lifestyle, and fashion niche, while TikTok leans more towards the entertainment and education niche. Likewise, LinkedIn is for business-to-business (B2B) folks, and Facebook is for e-commerce and local businesses.

Secure your digital infrastructure

In the digital age, one of the biggest threats businesses face is cyberattacks. If sensitive customer information is compromised, cyberattacks can damage customer trust, harm brand reputation, and lead to legal liabilities.

As cyber threats continue to evolve, small businesses need to prioritize security measures.

This includes securing websites with firewalls and SSL certificates, implementing strong passwords and multi-factor authentication, keeping software up to date, and securing the Wi-Fi network. If all this sounds way too technical, look upon a cyber security specialist to guide you.

If you've employees or contractors, train them to recognize phishing emails, avoid suspicious links, and follow data protection protocols. Here is a sample prompt to take ChatGPT's help to learn more:

Can you guide me on how to secure my digital infrastructure? I need advice on best practices for [specific area, e.g., data encryption, network security, user authentication, or backup strategies] to protect my business from potential cyber threats.

Track everything

The biggest benefit of using tech for running a business is every action can be tracked. By collecting and analyzing data, business owners can gain insights into customer behavior, marketing effectiveness, and sales trends.

Thus, implement analytics tools like Google Analytics, Crazy Egg, and CRM analytics software to track and measure the effectiveness of your initiatives. Then, take measures to optimize them. Here is how you can take ChatGPT's help:

Can you help me with strategies for analyzing customer data? I'm looking to understand [specific goal, e.g., customer behavior, purchasing trends, or segmentation] and how to use this data effectively to improve my business decisions and marketing efforts.

Using AI to Boost Productivity

Unless you live under a rock, you must have heard of AI and its game-changing capabilities. From writing detailed blogs to generating realistic images, AI is the new tech frontier. And like an astute business owner, you must get AI on your side and leverage it to the fullest.

I talked about how you can use AI for business planning in my last book. To reiterate, here are some areas where AI can help:

Content creation

Content is key for digital marketing, but creating high-quality content can be time-consuming and expensive. AI tools can generate content quickly and at a fraction of the cost.

Use AI writing tools like ChatGPT, Copy.ai, or Jasper to create blog posts, social media updates, product descriptions, and ad copy. These tools rely on natural language processing (NLP) to produce engaging content tailored to your audience. They all offer free plans, which are often enough for small businesses. Plus, the time saved by using these tools can quickly offset the subscription cost if you choose a paid plan.

Customer service

AI-powered chatbots can provide immediate responses to customer queries, offer support 24/7, and improve customer satisfaction without the need for a dedicated support team.

There are platforms like Tidio, ManyChat, or Intercom to automate basic customer interactions, such as answering frequently asked questions, guiding customers through a purchase, or scheduling appointments. Chatbots can also collect customer feedback and offer product recommendations, thereby enhancing the user experience.

Social media management

AI can also help you manage your social media accounts. It can streamline the process by automating content scheduling, engagement, and analytics. Tools like Hootsuite, Buffer, or Loomly utilize AI features to help you schedule posts, optimize posting times, and engage with followers automatically.

Financial management

Finance is essential to any business, and it's important to keep your venture on solid financial footing. While calculated risks can sometimes be beneficial, having a professional accountant on board greatly increases your ability to make informed financial decisions. Though some small businesses may find hiring an accountant challenging in the early stages, bringing one on as soon as possible can provide invaluable support and guidance that's well worth the investment.

While not a replacement for an accountant, AI tools can automate many aspects of accounting and financial tracking. Software like QuickBooks, Xero, or Wave can automate tasks such as invoicing, expense tracking, and financial reporting. These platforms can also generate insights into cash flow and profitability trends.

By staying on top of finances, you can make better decisions to keep your business afloat.

Task automation

Automation software can dramatically improve efficiency by handling repetitive tasks, freeing up valuable time for more strategic priorities. Tools like Zapier or IFTTT are excellent for automating workflows, such as sending emails, scheduling meetings, or updating CRM systems. These platforms connect with various business apps to perform tasks that would otherwise require manual effort.

AI-powered virtual assistants further enhance productivity by streamlining processes and analyzing data at remarkable speeds. When I started using virtual assistants with AI capabilities, their performance improved significantly. They became not only more efficient at routine tasks but also capable of assisting with creative and strategic work. With their ability to adapt and learn, these tools can help address challenges in smarter and more innovative ways.

While automation and AI tools offer incredible benefits, some may take time to master, so it's important to prepare for the learning involved. However, the payoff in terms of productivity is well worth the effort.

Wrap Up

You're now prepared to launch your business with confidence! This chapter covered the setup steps for home-based, brick-and-mortar, and online businesses, as well as tips for creating a functional workspace and choosing the right tech tools. You're almost ready to welcome your first customers.

Action Steps

1. Confirm the best setup for your business—whether home-based, physical,

or online.

2. Double-check all required permits, licenses, and insurance.

3. Get your workspace and essential tools ready for day one.

Up Next

In the next chapter, we're diving into digital marketing and branding. You'll learn how to create a standout online presence, develop a brand that sticks, and attract the right customers to grow your business.

Chapter Four

Mastering Digital Marketing and Brand Power

E very business owner knows for a fact that they need to market their business to succeed. The global digital advertising and marketing market in 2024 stands at $667 billion. And this is set to inflate to $786.2 billion by 2026 according to GlobalNewswire. This means more businesses are pumping out greater amounts of money to digital channels.

But do you know that 97% of internet marketing actually fails? Well, actually not. That's a popular internet myth, and no one's sure how much marketing money ends up failing. But one thing is for sure: just because you're spending money on marketing doesn't mean you're succeeding. You could be spending money on a losing cause and don't even know it.

Especially new business owners with little or no marketing knowledge, they're at a greater risk of burning up their hard-earned cash. I don't like to admit it, but been there and done that!

The good news is much of the failures are avoidable. With the right knowledge and the right direction, you can use digital marketing to your advantage, instead of a money pit.

In this chapter, we'll go over the basics of digital marketing and branding (arguably the most overused and misunderstood concept in marketing). In the first part, you'll learn about the various digital marketing channels and the core concept of branding.

The second part is hands-on, where you'll learn how to build an online presence from scratch and use AI in marketing.

By the end, you'll have a working knowledge of digital marketing to a point where you can carry it out on your own or hire a marketer and keep them accountable so that they don't throw your money down the drain.

Digital Marketing Fundamentals: Kept Simple for Non-Marketers

The road to mastery starts with mastering the fundamentals. So, let's start at the very basics.

Note that digital marketing is an overarching term and comprises of various components. Some components are linked, while others are not. In this section, I'll list the core concepts of digital marketing along with its components.

In addition to that, there are a few other things that need explanations: branding, marketing, and advertising. These are often used interchangeably, which is not only misleading but also dangerous. You'll come across these terms in the rest of the book. So, it's important you know what they mean and don't mean.

Understanding Brand

Imagine you walk into a store with a large collection of wine. You stroll through the selection, inspecting the bottles randomly. Suddenly, a purple-hued bottle with an unusual shape catches your eye. You can't help but pick the bottle up, look at the label, and check its features and packaging. Impressed by the design, you head over the counter to buy it.

That's what a brand does. It helps a product stand out from the rest.

A brand is much more than just your business name, logo, or slogan—it's the overall image and feeling that people associate with your business. It's how your customers see you and what they think of when they hear your name or see your products.

When someone suggests you need to "brand" your business or invest in "branding," they mean creating an emotional connection or association with your company name. If it's about you personally, it refers to building a personal brand.

Phil Knight and the Power of "Why"

This concept of brand goes deeper than just appearance or messaging. It's about connecting with people on an emotional level, which is exactly what Nike's founder, Phil Knight, did during a keynote speech. Instead of talking about Nike's cutting-edge technologies or their celebrity endorsements, he told a story about the runners who get up at 5 a.m., no matter how cold or wet the weather is, and push themselves to do their best.

He asked the audience, "If you run at least once a week, stand up." Then, he narrowed it down: "If you run 2-3 times a week, regardless of the weather, keep standing." By the end, only a few people remained standing. He pointed to them and said, "We are for you. When you get up to run in the cold and wet, we're standing out there with you, cheering you on. We're the inner athlete. We're the inner champion."

Without mentioning the latest product features or which athletes wear their gear, Knight powerfully connected Nike's brand to something deeper—the "why" behind it all. Nike's "Just Do It" is more than a slogan; it's a rallying cry for those who push through adversity to be their best.

The 'Why' Behind the Brand

People are not drawn to what you do; they are attracted to why you do it. This is the true differentiator in any business, career, or life. Just like Nike, your brand must connect on a deeper level with your audience. You can either wander through life hoping for something to connect or you can go through it with intention, knowing your 'why,' and heading straight to where you belong.

If you want to create a brand people can truly relate to, if you want them to feel passionate about your product, service, or even you as a person, it starts with knowing your 'why.' Your brand should embody that purpose and resonate with others in a way that's impossible to ignore.

Marketing vs Advertising

Another misconception most people outside of the marketing world have is marketing and advertising is the same. But there's an important subtle difference.

Marketing is all about the activities you do to get people interested in your product or service. It includes everything you do to understand your customers, tell your story, and attract potential buyers to your business.

Advertising is a part of marketing. It's the specific action of promoting your products or services through paid methods. Take note of the word "paid". Advertising means placing an ad somewhere—like in a local newspaper, on social media, or on a billboard—to make people aware of your brand or encourage them to buy something.

Marketing helps people know you exist, while advertising lets you directly tell them, through paid mediums, about your products.

With the definitions out of the way, let's dive into digital marketing.

So, what is digital marketing? Digital marketing is simply marketing your products or services using the internet. It's how you promote your business online, using tools like websites, social media, emails, and search engines to reach people.

With the rise of the internet, most people are now more engaged in online channels than offline channels. A report by eMarketer reveals the majority of consumers worldwide prefer searching online over in-store for certain categories like electronics, clothes, toys, books, and more. As a result, a significant portion of marketing budgets is now directed toward digital marketing channels.

The conclusion is this: as a business owner, you simply cannot ignore digital marketing.

As already said, digital marketing is an all-encompassing term and it consists of various components. These are:

- SEO

- PPC

- Content marketing

- Social media marketing

- Email marketing

- Affiliate marketing

- Video marketing

- Audio marketing

Let's unpack each component in more detail.

SEO or Search Engine Optimization

Recall the last time you wanted to learn more about something. What did you do? Chances are you Googled that thing. Googled is colloquial for "searching the internet." In this digital world, acquiring knowledge starts with a search.

Search Engine Optimization (SEO) is the process of improving your website so that it ranks higher in search engine results, like on Google. When people search for something related to your business, SEO helps make sure they find your website first. The goal is to get your website to show up near the top of the search results so more people visit it.

Google holds 90% of the search market. And ranking higher on Google is the #1 priority for most businesses.

PPC or Pay-per-Click

PPC or Pay-Per-Click is a type of online advertising where you pay each time someone clicks on your ad. In PPC advertising, you create an ad, set a budget, and choose keywords or target settings to decide who sees your ad. Platforms like Google Ads,

Facebook Ads, or Instagram Ads allow you to show your ads to people who are likely to be interested in your products or services.

In Google, these ads appear at the top of search engine results pages, marked as "Ad." If someone searches for "best bakery in Louisville" on Google, they might see your bakery's ad at the top of the search results. Search ads are effective for reaching people actively looking for something specific. Likewise, social media ads are shown to people based on their interests, demographics, or behavior.

Content Marketing

Content marketing is a form of marketing where you use content to gain awareness and generate leads for your business. The content can be blog posts, books whitepapers, videos, reports, or anything that contains information.

The idea behind content marketing is to provide content that your potential customers find useful, interesting, or entertaining. When people see that your content adds value to their life, they're more likely to trust your brand and eventually buy from you. In fact, content marketing is said to generate 3x as many leads as outbound marketing (where you reach out to customers) at 62% less cost!

Social Media Marketing

An estimated 5.17 billion people are on social media, accounting for 67% of the world population. A large number of people will be joining the bandwagon soon. Social media marketing is about using social platforms like Facebook, Instagram, TikTok, LinkedIn, and Twitter to promote your business.

At its core, social media marketing is about creating content that your audience finds interesting or entertaining—and sharing it in the places where they already spend their time. The goal is to build a community around your brand, one that is active, engaged, and that feels a genuine connection to your business.

Email Marketing

Email is the old-school way of marketing your business cost-effectively. The top email marketers generate $36 for every $1 spent, making email one of the most effective marketing channels!

Email marketing involves sending targeted messages to a group of subscribers—people who have willingly signed up to receive updates from your business. These messages can range from newsletters to special offers, product announcements, event invitations, or educational content.

The biggest benefit of email marketing is its reach. Unlike social media, where algorithms determine how many people see your posts, email marketing allows you to reach your subscribers directly in their inboxes. This makes it one of the most reliable ways to get your message across.

Video Marketing

Video marketing is a powerful way to connect with your audience and promote your business using videos. It lets you tell stories through moving images and sound. With platforms like YouTube and Facebook Live, videos are now more popular than text. And with smartphones and free editing tools, the cost of creating and distributing videos is at an all time low.

You can use different types of videos like user-generated videos, product demos, behind-the-scenes videos, animated videos, etc.

Audio Marketing

Along with videos, audio has also grown more mainstream. With platforms like Spotify, Apple Music, and Podbean, creators and businesses can host and broadcast audio. Besides podcasts, there are audiobooks and voice assistants like Siri, which allow businesses to get in front of users through audio. Audio content can make your content more accessible to people with visual impairments. If that's a niche you're in, take audio marketing seriously.

Affiliate Marketing

Affiliate marketing is a different form of marketing where you don't do the marketing yourself. Instead, you contract with others who send you leads and customers for a fee. These contractors are known as affiliates. These are the people or companies who promote your products or services. They can be bloggers, influencers, other businesses, or even customers who love what you do.

Affiliates use special tracking links to promote their products. When someone clicks on the link and makes a purchase (or completes another desired action, like signing up for a newsletter), the affiliate earns a commission.

When done correctly, affiliate marketing can ensure a steady stream of customers for your new business.

Note that digital marketing is a dynamic field that is constantly evolving. New marketing mediums and channels are emerging regularly, offering businesses innovative ways to reach and engage their target audience. This rapid pace of change is driven by technological advancements, shifting consumer behaviors, and changing regulatory environments. So stay updated with the changing times and incorporate the most effective marketing mediums.

Creating a Strong Brand Identity

We'll get started with digital marketing in the next section. But there's a prerequisite. And that is to create a strong brand identity.

I'll stress its importance with an example. Let's say a weight loss business runs a marketing campaign across different digital marketing channels. It runs PPC, video ads, SEO campaigns, and a podcast. In the PPC, it runs text-based ads that claim to help you lose weight through lemon juice. In the video ad, the ad features a nanny gaining weight through a meat-rich diet. In SEO, it ranks for dog food, and the podcast features swimming lessons.

Now unless the different concepts are connected to weight loss, the audience is likely to get confused as to what the business wants to convey. As Meridith Elliott Powell said, "The Confused Mind Never Buys". Hence, if your brand is not clear, it may come as a turnoff.

That's why creating a strong brand identity that's consistent across all digital channels is crucial. Consistent branding helps build trust with potential customers. When people see that your brand has a cohesive look, feel, and tone across all touchpoints, they perceive it as more professional and reliable. Trust is particularly important for small businesses, as consumers often choose brands they feel comfortable with.

A well-crafted brand identity helps your audience recognize your business immediately.

So, how do you create a strong brand identity? That's a task easier said than done. But with the right approach, you can create one. Here are the key components of a brand identity:

- Brand name - A memorable and relevant name that reflects your business's essence.

- Logo - A visually appealing symbol that represents your brand and is easily recognizable.

- Tagline - A catchy phrase that captures the essence of your brand and is memorable.

- Brand story - A compelling narrative that explains your business's purpose, values, and mission.

- Visual identity - The overall look and feel of your brand, including colors, typography, and imagery.

- Tone of voice - The way your brand communicates with customers, whether it's formal, informal, or humorous.

- Brand personality - The unique character or personality that your brand projects.

- Brand values - The core principles and beliefs that guide your business's decisions and actions.

- Brand experience - The overall impression customers have of your brand, from their initial interaction to their post-purchase experience.

- Brand messaging - The key messages that you want to communicate to your target audience.

When creating a brand experience, take note of two things: target audience and authenticity. Will your target market appreciate a business that comes off as aggressive/soothing/cheerful/alarming? And will you be able to wear that personality for the rest of your business life? Remember, authenticity matters just as much as the products and the personality and values. If you're not authentic, you'll soon find yourself in a startup graveyard, a place for failed new businesses.

Looking Upon Freelancers to Assist You With Your Brand

Freelancers have been incredibly valuable to me, offering a flexible and affordable way to accomplish tasks without the need for full-time employees. Whether you're tackling a one-time project or need ongoing support, freelancers bring specialized skills that can save you time and money. Here's a look at what freelancers can do, how to hire the right one, and what you can expect to pay.

What Freelancers Can Do

Freelancers are skilled specialists who let you pay only for the specific services you need. Here's a quick breakdown of some of what they offer:

- Graphic Design & Branding

Need a logo, website, or marketing materials? Freelancers can bring your vision to life. Platforms like 99Designs are perfect for this, as you can run design contests and get multiple ideas from different designers. It's like having a creative team at your fingertips!

- Writing & Content Creation

Freelancers can write everything from blog posts and social media updates to newsletters and entire ebooks. They can also help optimize your content for search engines, so your brand gets noticed.

- Web Development & Maintenance

Building a website or need someone to maintain your existing one? Freelance developers are here to help, whether it's a small tweak or a full-scale redesign.

- Marketing & Social Media

Need help with SEO or running a digital marketing campaign? Freelancers can manage your online presence, including social media accounts, so you can focus on running your business.

- Admin & Virtual Assistance

From data entry to calendar management, freelancers can handle the behind-the-scenes tasks that free up your time to focus on what really matters.

Tips for Hiring Freelancers

- Know what you need: Before you start looking, get clear on your project's goals, timeline, and budget. The more specific you are, the easier it will be to find the right person for the job.

- Check their work: Take the time to look at a freelancer's portfolio or past work. It'll give you a sense of their style and abilities. Don't forget to read client reviews—these are often the best indicators of how reliable they are.

- Set expectations: Be upfront about what you expect—project scope, deadlines, and payment terms. This helps avoid misunderstandings down the road.

- Start small: If you're unsure about a freelancer, consider starting with a smaller project first. It's a great way to test the waters before committing to something bigger.

- Time zones matter: If the freelancer's in a different time zone, it's important to align on working hours and communication expectations. It helps prevent delays and ensures smooth collaboration.

What Freelancers Charge

Freelance rates vary widely based on experience, location, and the type of work. Here's a general guide to what you can expect to pay:

Graphic Design:

- Low: $15–$35 per hour (newbies or offshore designers)

- Mid: $35–$75 per hour (experienced designers with a solid portfolio)

- High: $75–$150+ per hour (high-end designers or specialists)

Content Writing:

- Low: $0.05–$0.10 per word (entry-level or general content)

- Mid: $0.10–$0.30 per word (more experienced writers with niche expertise)

- High: $0.30–$1.00+ per word (top-tier writers or specialized content)

Web Development:

- Low: $25–$50 per hour (junior developers or offshore)

- Mid: $50–$100 per hour (experienced developers with strong portfolios)

- High: $100–$200+ per hour (specialized or senior developers)

Digital Marketing:

- Low: $15–$30 per hour (beginner or offshore marketers)

- Mid: $30–$75 per hour (mid-level marketers with proven success)

- High: $75–$150+ per hour (highly experienced consultants)

Building an Online Presence

We're done with the first part, which was theoretical knowledge. Now let's begin the second part, which is implementing the acquired knowledge to build an online presence.

Irrespective of whether you're a home-based business, online business or a brick-and-mortar business, it's imperative to build an online presence. Establishing an effective online presence involves several steps, each leveraging digital marketing techniques to reach and engage the right audience. Here's a step-by-step guide on how to do it:

Define your brand identity

If you haven't already, you need to define the brand identity first. Otherwise, you'll be essentially flushing your marketing money down the drain.

Take a sheet of paper (or open a notepad if you're on PC) and note down the following:

- Brand purpose: Why does your business exist? What problem does it solve?

- Target audience: Who are your ideal customers? Understand their needs, preferences, and online behavior.

- Brand voice and personality: Establish a consistent tone for communication—whether it's friendly, formal, playful, etc.

- Visual identity: Include elements like a logo, color palette, fonts, and design style that represent your brand and will be used across all digital channels.

Here is a sample to help you get started:

Prompt:

Can you help me define my brand identity for my business? I need guidance on establishing a strong foundation by identifying:
  - *Brand purpose: Why my business exists and the problem it solves*

  - *Target audience: Who my ideal customers are and their needs, prefer-*

> *ences, and online behavior*
>
> - *Brand voice and personality: The tone I should consistently use, like friendly, formal, or playful*
>
> - *Visual identity: Key elements like a logo, color palette, fonts, and design style to use across digital channels*
>
> *I want to make sure this is clear before starting my marketing strategy.*

Include this at the top of every digital marketing strategy and report to help you stay on track.

Create a website

Your website is your business's primary online home. It's your business's digital address. Therefore, you must invest in a website that speaks to your brand's image and personality.

You can use free platforms like WordPress or SaaS tools like Shopify, Wix, and Site123 to build a website. Whatever your choice, here are the things to focus on:

- Domain and hosting: Domain is the name of your website (Google.com, Amazon.com), while hosting is the cloud server where your website will be hosted.

- Design and functionality: Build a professional, mobile-friendly website that aligns with your brand identity. Platforms like Shopify, WordPress, or Wix make it easy to design a website for non-technical users.

- User experience (UX): Ensure your website is easy to navigate, loads quickly, and has clear calls to action (e.g., "Buy Now," "Contact Us").

- E-commerce capability: If you're selling products, set up an e-commerce platform that allows customers to browse and purchase easily.

It's important not to spend too much time and money on creating the website. You can hire a freelancer on Fiverr, Freelancer, or Upwork, and get a professional-looking website for as little as $200.

Optimize your website with SEO

SEO, or Search Engine Optimization, is the process of improving a website so it ranks higher in search engine results (like Google). The goal is to make the site more visible to people searching for related topics, which can bring in more visitors. It involves using relevant keywords, creating quality content, and ensuring the site runs smoothly.

Once you have your website ready, time to drive internet users to it, and you can do it through SEO. One of the benefits of SEO is its organic traffic, which means users are actively looking for certain products or services. Thus, this traffic has a higher conversion rate.

When you optimize your website for search engines like Google, you increase its chances of appearing higher in search results for relevant keywords. This means more people are likely to find your website and learn about your business.

Note that SEO is a specialized process that requires research, content, optimization, and maintenance. Therefore, if you don't have the required time, skills and knowledge, it'd be better if you could hire SEO experts to handle the task for you. Platforms like Fiverr and Freelancer have experienced contractors that will do it for you, at an affordable price.

Develop a content marketing strategy

Content marketing is a strategy where businesses create and share valuable, relevant content (like articles, videos, or social media posts) to attract and engage their target audience. Instead of directly promoting a product, it focuses on providing helpful information or entertainment, building trust and brand awareness, which can lead to sales over time.

Content marketing is arguably the best way to get traffic to your website consistently. By providing valuable content, you position yourself as an expert in your field, building trust and credibility with your audience. This is especially important for new businesses.

Therefore, develop and implement a content marketing strategy. Here are the things involved in content marketing:

- Target audience identification - Clearly define who you want to reach with your content.

- Content research – Research what kind of content you can create and what the competition is like.

- Content creation - Develop a variety of content formats, such as blog posts, articles, videos, infographics, and social media posts.

- Content distribution - Determine the best channels to distribute your content, such as your website, social media, email marketing, and guest blogging.

- Content promotion: Use paid and organic methods to promote your content and reach a wider audience.

Just like SEO, content marketing requires the eye of an expert. Content marketers specialize in this field and can implement the strategy for you.

Run ads to acquire customers faster

SEO and content marketing are great, but one of the disadvantages with them is they take time to produce results.

Arguably, the fastest way to get customers for a new business is by running ads. Digital platforms like Google and Facebook allow you to set up and run targeted ads to acquire customers with a minimal marketing budget.

While the specific steps to run ads vary by the platform, here are some common steps:

- Define your target audience: Identify the specific demographics, interests, and behaviors of your ideal customers.

- Create compelling ad copy and visuals: Write persuasive ad copy and design eye-catching visuals.

- Set your budget: Determine how much you're willing to spend on your ad campaign.

- Track and optimize: Monitor the performance of your ads and make adjustments as needed to improve your results.

Running ads is also an activity that's best left to experts. Thus, hire a digital ads expert from platforms like Upwork and Freelancer to get the best ROI for you.

Leverage email marketing

Email marketing is a high ROI-producing marketing medium. And it is an effective way to nurture leads and keep your audience engaged.

Here's how to do email marketing for your business:

- Build an email list: Use lead magnets like discounts, free ebooks, or exclusive content to encourage visitors to subscribe to your email list. Place signup forms prominently on your website and social media channels.

- Nurture campaigns: Create email campaigns that keep subscribers informed about new products, promotions, or useful content. Platforms like Mailchimp or ConvertKit allow you to design and automate these emails.

- Personalization: Segment your email list based on customer interests or behavior to make your emails more personalized and relevant, which will increase open rates and conversions.

Emails work well with your website and paid ads. When someone shows interest in your business (a "lead"), it's important to build a connection with them before they're ready to buy. Regular, helpful emails can keep them engaged and increase the chance they'll become a paying customer.

Partner with affiliates

As already said, affiliate marketing involves partnering with other businesses and individuals to promote your products or services. This is a great way to get customers without doing the marketing yourself.

If suitable, consider creating an affiliate program. Look for businesses or individuals who have a relevant audience and can promote your products or services effectively. You can sign up for platforms like ClickBank to list your affiliate program and find affiliates for your new business.

Track, analyze, optimize

Last but not least, you need to track every marketing activity and optimize for performance. Tracking is the only way to know if your marketing dollars are producing leads. There are both free tools like Google Analytics and paid tools like SproutSocial, which enable tracking marketing campaigns. If you're planning to outsource marketing, make sure to ask for reports on a weekly basis. Accountability is the only way to avoid wasting money on marketing.

Using AI for Marketing and Brand Development

Before 2023, it was understandable if you hadn't incorporated AI into your marketing efforts. But by 2024, it's almost unthinkable.

The introduction of ChatGPT in 2023 brought a groundbreaking tool for businesses. It can produce content, create business and marketing plans, manage basic accounting tasks, and even write code. Skipping AI now means missing many opportunities.

For beginners, my books "Prompt Engineering and ChatGPT" and "ChatGPT for Business" offer easy-to-follow guidance on using AI in your business, helping you tap into AI's full potential.

Here's what you can use AI for in your marketing:

Generating marketing plans

AI tools like ChatGPT can create marketing plans for your business from scratch. All you have to do is provide a prompt and let ChatGPT create a thorough plan. A prompt is nothing but the information you input to AI tools.

For generating a marketing plan, a prompt can look something like this:

"I'm starting an online business that specializes in [niche]. I'll be offering [products], primarily through my website. My audience is [target market]. I plan to market through [marketing channels] with a budget of [marketing budget]. Create a detailed marketing plan for me."

If you input the text in ChatGPT, you'll get a detailed response:

Prompt:

I'm starting an online business that specializes in the online sweaters niche. I'll be offering hand-knit sweaters, primarily through my website. My audience is working women who need sweaters for the office. I plan to market through TikTok and Facebook with a budget of $10,000. Create a detailed marketing plan for me.

Output:

Executive Summary

This marketing plan outlines a strategic approach to launch and promote your online hand-knit sweaters business targeting working women who need stylish and comfortable sweaters for the office. With a budget of $10,000 and a focus on TikTok and Facebook for marketing, this plan aims to build brand awareness, drive website traffic, and generate sales through a combination of organic and paid marketing strategies.

1. Business Overview

- **Product**: Hand-knit sweaters designed for professional women.

- **Sales Channel**: Primarily through your dedicated website.

- **Unique Selling Proposition (USP)**: High-quality, stylish, and comfortable sweaters that blend professionalism with personal style, hand-knit to ensure uniqueness and quality.

2. Market Analysis
2.1 Industry Overview
- **Market Growth**: The global sweater market is experiencing steady growth, with increasing demand for artisanal and sustainable fashion.

- **Trends**:

  - **Sustainability**: Consumers prefer ethically made products.

  - **Artisanal Products**: Growing appreciation for handcrafted items.

  - **Workplace Fashion**: Demand for professional yet stylish office attire.

2.2 Competitor Analysis
- **Direct Competitors**:

  - Other online retailers offering hand-knit or artisanal sweaters.

- **Indirect Competitors**:

  - Mass-produced sweater brands targeting professional women.

- **Competitive Advantage**:

  - Hand-knit uniqueness.

  - Personalization options.

  - Storytelling around craftsmanship.

(Continues on)

Allocating marketing budget

You can ask ChatGPT to allocate the marketing budget across various channels.

A good prompt for this can be:

"My marketing budget is [budget]. I want to develop a WordPress website, start a YouTube channel, run Facebook and TikTok ads, and an email campaign using MailChimp. Allocate the marketing budget accordingly."

Prompt:

My marketing budget is $5,000. I want to develop a WordPress website, start a YouTube channel, run Facebook and TikTok ads, and an email campaign using MailChimp. Allocate the marketing budget accordingly.

Output:

With a marketing budget of $5,000, we can create a well-balanced approach that covers building your website, setting up and promoting your YouTube channel, running Facebook and TikTok ads, and launching email campaigns with MailChimp. Here's how to allocate the budget:

Budget Breakdown:

1. **WordPress Website Development:** $1,500

2. **YouTube Channel Setup & Content Creation:** $1,000

3. **Facebook & TikTok Ads:** $2,000

4. **MailChimp Email Campaign:** $500

WordPress Website Development ($1,500)Purpose: Establish a professional online storefront for your hand-knit sweaters, where visitors can browse products, learn about your brand, and make purchases.

(Continues on)

Generating content

AI tools are really good at creating content on par with a human writer. Thus, you can use this capability to create content for your website, YouTube channel, ebooks, product demos, landing pages, etc.

Here's a prompt for this purpose:

"My new business's name is [business name]. The business specializes in [niche] and caters to [target audience]. Myself [name] and I'm the owner of the company with [specialization and experience]. My business solves [the problem]. Based on the information, create an About Us section for my website."

Prompt:

My new business's name is Tara Sweaters. The business specializes in hand-knit sweaters and caters to working women. I'm Tara Smith the owner of the company with 10 years of expertise in the fashion business. My business aims to make sweaters trendier again. Based on the information, create an About Us section for my website.

Output:

About Us:

Welcome to Tara Sweaters!

I'm Tara Smith, the founder of Tara Sweaters, and I've spent over a decade in the fashion industry perfecting my craft. My passion for timeless style and hand-crafted quality led me to create Tara Sweaters—a brand dedicated to making sweaters trendier again for the modern working woman.

At Tara Sweaters, we believe that office wear can be both comfortable and fashionable. Our hand-knit sweaters are designed to add a touch of warm elegance, and trendiness to your everyday work wardrobe. Each piece is crafted with care, combining classic techniques with contemporary styles to create garments that are both unique and versatile.

Optimizing content for SEO

You can instruct ChatGPT to make the content SEO friendly. All you have to do is specify the main keyword (A *keyword* is a word or phrase that people type into search engines (like Google) when they're looking for specific information, products, or services), related keywords, and the keyword density. ChatGPT will handle the request accordingly.

A follow-up prompt example could be: *"Now optimize the About Us page for "[main keyword]" as the main keyword, and "[secondary keyword]" as the secondary keyword. Keep the keyword density at 3%."*

Prompt:

Now optimize the About Us page for "trendy sweaters" as the main keyword, and "sweaters for winters" as the secondary keyword. Keep the keyword density at 3%.

Output:

About Us

Welcome to Tara Sweaters, where trendy sweaters meet timeless style!

I'm Tara Smith, the founder of Tara Sweaters, with over 10 years of experience in the fashion industry. My passion for quality and handcrafted design led me to create Tara Sweaters—a brand dedicated to making trendy sweaters that cater to the needs of working women. We believe that office wear can be both comfortable and fashionable, and our trendy sweaters are crafted to fit seamlessly into your work wardrobe.

Creating SOPs to outsource marketing activities

An SOP (Standard Operating Procedure) is a detailed, written document that outlines the steps to complete a specific task or process consistently and efficiently. It ensures uniformity, compliance, and quality in operations across an organization.

As your business grows, you may feel the need to hire marketers to handle the marketing activities for you. But hiring is not the end-all-be-all of marketing. You need to negotiate with them and keep them accountable. And ChatGPT can help you in this regard.

Here's a prompt you can use:

"I'm planning to hire a [marketing domain]. Create a SOP that I can share with him and keep him accountable."

Prompt:

I'm planning to hire a Google Ads expert. Create a SOP that I can share with him and keep him accountable.

Output:

Standard Operating Procedure (SOP) for Google Ads Expert
Objective: To manage and optimize Google Ads campaigns effectively, ensuring optimal use of the budget, increased conversions, and a positive return on investment (ROI).
Role and Responsibilities:
  1. **Account Setup and Management**

- Set up the Google Ads account, including linking Google Analytics and conversion tracking.

- Ensure accurate billing and access permissions.

- Regularly update and manage account settings for optimal performance.

(Continues on)

These are just some of the ways AI can aid your marketing efforts. As your business grows, you can ask it to act as a virtual assistant and perform mundane tasks like updating the marketing plan, checking for compliance, and generating ROI reports.

Paid AI tools are even more beneficial. Thus, explore the possibilities and use AI to your advantage.

Wrap Up

This chapter gave you a deep dive into digital marketing fundamentals, from building brand identity to mastering channels like SEO, social media, and content marketing. With a clear brand and marketing strategy, you're ready to make a lasting impression on your audience.

Action Steps

1. Define your brand's core message and design a look that reflects your values.

2. Choose a few digital channels to focus on first, like social media or email.

3. Develop a simple marketing plan to guide your early campaigns and start building brand awareness.

Up Next

Next, we'll get into the heart of customer acquisition. Learn to identify your target market, hone your sales approach, and turn potential leads into loyal clients—setting you up for lasting growth.

Chapter Five

Smart Money Moves

A s a small business owner, I've felt the pressure to scale quickly. It's easy to get swept up in the excitement of expansion, to dream of what could be when the numbers grow and opportunities flood in.

I've learned through experience that pursuing growth purely for its own sake can be risky. In my case, it came at a significant cost to both myself and my business. I found myself constantly chasing the next goal without stopping to assess whether I was truly prepared. It's like pushing forward faster than your legs can handle, hoping not to stumble.

Wag, the dog-walking startup, is a perfect example of what happens when growth outpaces the foundation of a business. In its early days, Wag was an ambitious idea—"Uber for dogs"—and it gained significant venture capital funding to scale quickly. But as the company grew, it became clear that the focus on speed and size was far more important than building a sustainable business. And that's when things started falling apart.

Instead of focusing on the problems in their business model, Wag pushed forward with global expansion, hiring a new CEO, Hilary Schneider, to handle the growth. But as the company expanded, the cracks started to show. Wag relied heavily on independent contractors to provide the service, but they had no system for vetting or training them properly. And as the volume grew, so did the incidents: lost dogs, abuse, even deaths. Customer service couldn't keep up, and the reputation began to crumble.

The worst part? The people running the company weren't listening. They were too focused on being the next unicorn. They wanted to be big, but they didn't have the foundation to support it. And when thousands of workers sued for misclassification, the company was forced to face the consequences of not taking care of its people or its business.

Wag's story is a painful reminder of the dangers of chasing growth without thinking through the long-term impact. In the end, despite the flashy funding and the desire to become a household name, the company wasn't sustainable. It was a lesson in the brutal reality of blitzscaling—where scaling too fast and too big can unravel everything you've built.

However, this doesn't mean that funding is not important. Lack of capital is one of the main reasons new businesses fail. Cash flow is the lifeblood of any business. When the funds runs out, operations shut down and the business fails.

In the nascent stages of a startup, capital acts as a catalyst for innovation and ex-perimentation. It provides the necessary resources to develop new products, hire talented individuals, and explore uncharted territories. As Peter Drucker famously stated, *"Innovation is not about technology. It's about people and ideas."* Capital en-ables startups to assemble the right teams and nurture the creative minds that drive groundbreaking business ideas.

The importance of money doesn't surface when you build a team. Even when you're going solo, you'll realize the importance of having money in the bank to fund operations.

In other words, take money flow seriously from day 1 of your business, irrespective of the team or operation size. That's why this chapter is important.

Chapter 5 is dedicated to ensuring your newly started business stays healthy fi-nancially. We'll go over the various funding options available, especially for a small business owner. Some are more easily accessible than others. But you should know that they exist.

In the second part of this chapter, we'll delve deeper into financial forecasting. This is to help you calculate how much money you'll actually be needed to run your business. Both under and over-funding are bad for business health. Again, we'll be using the latest AI techniques in this regard. There are various specialized tools that have made financial forecasting easier, more accurate, and affordable.

So grab your favorite drink, and let's dive in.

10 Ways to Fund a New Venture

The landscape of entrepreneurship has undergone a dramatic transformation, with access to capital becoming more accessible than ever before. In the past, obtaining funding was often a daunting and time-consuming process, requiring extensive documentation, collateral, and a proven track record. Banks were notoriously conservative, often hesitant to lend to startups with limited financial histories.

Over time, a confluence of factors, including technological advancements, regulatory changes, and increased investor interest, has democratized the funding process. Today, a plethora of options are available.

Of course, not all of the funding options are suitable for a particular business. The job of the founder is to determine the best sources and secure the funding.

There are over 15 ways to fund a business, typically grouped into three categories:

- Self-funding

- Investor funding

- Loans

Self-funding is when you use your own money to bring in liquidity. Note that self-funding also includes money borrowed from friends and family. Investor funding is when you bring in investors to your business and they provide the financing. Lastly, there's a loan which is often issued by a bank or financial institution.

Now that you know about the types, let's go over the 10 most common funding options for new businesses.

1. Personal Savings: Start with What You Have

2. Credit Cards: Lifeline or Trap?

3. Friends and Family: Your First Supporters

4. Personal Loans: Pros and Cons

5. Crowdfunding: Turn the Crowd into Investors

6. Angel Investors: Life Savers?

7. Venture Capital: A Step Up

8. SBA Loans: The Small Business Option

9. Business Line of Credit: Flexible Funding

10. Grants: The Power of Free Funding

Personal Savings

Many businesses start with personal funding, where the founder uses their own savings to kick-start the venture. It's a straightforward and quick way to finance a business.

For example, Sara Blakely, founder of Spanx, used her personal savings of $5,000 from her job as a door-to-door salesperson. With this initial capital, she created prototypes, filed a patent, and found a manufacturer, ultimately building Spanx into a billion-dollar company.

Pros

- Fast and easy to access

- Full ownership (no equity dilution)

- No interest or repayment obligations

Cons

- Limited by personal savings

- Personal financial risk if the business fails

- May limit funding available for growth

Credit Cards

Credit cards are a common tool for startup funding, offering immediate access to funds. Many entrepreneurs share stories of using credit cards to cover initial expenses. One advantage is the flexibility to borrow only what's needed up to the credit limit, helping bridge cash flow gaps.

Pros

- Quick access to funds

- Flexible borrowing up to credit limit

- Useful for short-term expenses

Cons

- High interest rates, if not paid off monthly

- Can lead to debt accumulation if the business struggles

- Not ideal for long-term or major funding needs

Friends and Family

Funding from family and friends is a common early-stage option. They may offer support as loans, gifts, or equity investments, providing both financial help and emotional encouragement. However, it's essential to manage expectations to avoid strain on personal relationships carefully.

Pros

- Flexible terms (low or no interest, relaxed terms)

- Emotional support from trusted individuals

- No strict repayment schedules

Cons

- Potential strain on personal relationships

- Risk of losing both financial support and trust

- May limit future funding options if significant capital is required

Personal Loans

Personal loans allow founders to borrow based on personal credit, often without requiring a business income history. These loans provide lump sums that can cover startup costs, but they also hold the founder personally liable if the business does not succeed.

Pros

- No need for an established business history

- Fixed payments and interest rates

- Useful for initial costs like inventory

Cons

- Personal liability if the business fails

- May have higher interest rates than business loans

- Limited by personal creditworthiness

Crowdfunding

Crowdfunding platforms like Kickstarter allow businesses to raise funds from the public, often in exchange for rewards or early product access. For instance, Oculus VR used Kickstarter to raise nearly $2.5 million, surpassing its initial goal of $250,000 and gaining significant traction in the tech community.

Pros

- No repayment obligation if the business fails

- Engages public interest, often building a customer base

- Can offer rewards instead of equity

Cons

- Highly competitive; not all campaigns succeed

- Limited funds for businesses with less public appeal

- Typically, a one-time funding solution

Angel Investors

Angel investors provide early-stage funding in exchange for equity, often bringing valuable industry experience. This can be crucial for product development and early marketing. Angels are valuable mentors but can be selective about where they invest.

Pros

- Access to significant early capital

- Mentorship and strategic guidance

- No repayment obligation

Cons

- Equity dilution (part of the business ownership)

- Finding suitable investors can be challenging

- Investors may have input in business decisions

Venture Capital

Venture capital (VC) firms invest in businesses with high growth potential, often through funding rounds (Series A, B, etc.). For example, Airbnb secured early VC support from Sequoia Capital, helping it scale rapidly.

Pros

- Large amounts of funding

- Support with scaling and strategic growth

- Access to networks and resources

Cons

- Significant equity dilution

- Complex approval and selection process

- Pressure to meet high growth expectations

SBA Loans

The U.S. Small Business Administration (SBA) offers loans backed by the government, making them less risky for lenders and often more affordable for borrowers. SBA loans require extensive documentation but provide long-term, lower-cost financing.

Pros

- Favorable terms due to government backing

- Good for larger, long-term funding needs

- Supportive of various business types

Cons

- Extensive paperwork and time-consuming process

- Requires good credit to qualify

- Strict usage restrictions

Grants

Grants are non-repayable funds from governments or nonprofits, often awarded to innovative or socially beneficial projects. Ginkgo Bioworks, for example, received a $100,000 grant from the Department of Energy for bioengineering.

Pros

- No repayment required

- May offer substantial funding amounts

- Support for innovative and community-focused projects

Cons

- Highly competitive application process

- Often restricted on how funds can be used

- Limited to certain industries or initiatives

Business Line of Credit

A business line of credit functions like a flexible loan, allowing companies to borrow up to a certain limit and repay as needed. It's ideal for covering short-term expenses like payroll or inventory and provides a revolving source of capital.

Pros

- Flexible and revolving credit source

- Good for managing cash flow

- Borrow only what's needed

Cons

- May have higher interest rates for smaller businesses

- Can lead to debt if not managed responsibly

- May require good business or personal credit

Each funding source has unique advantages and limitations. Consider your startup's needs, growth stage, and risk tolerance to choose the best option for success.

Financial Forecasting: How Much Money Will You Need?

You know about the sources of funding. Based on your skillset and current situation, you're likely to trigger a mix of funding sources.

But there's a bigger question lurking. That is, how much should I raise? Will $100,000 be enough? Or will I have to secure a $300,000 loan deal?

Both under and over-funding are bad for new business. In under-funding, you're at the risk of running out of money before turning profitable. Over-funded businesses often end up taking a lot of initiatives, most of which end up failing. That's why it's important to know how much to raise.

You can answer this question through financial forecasting.

Financial forecasting is essentially the practice of predicting future financial conditions and performance based on historical data, market trends, and other relevant factors. It helps business owners anticipate their financial needs, set realistic goals, make informed decisions, and plan for both short-term operations and long-term growth.

While forecasting is often employed by big corporates, it's equally important for small enterprises. Small businesses often operate with limited resources, which means that financial stability is vital for survival. Small businesses can face fluctuating sales based on local events, seasonal demand, and customer preferences.

The Financial Forecast Process

As a business owner, you should have a birds-eye view of the financial forecasting process even if you're not a finance person. This helps you ensure the financial viability of your new venture.

The process of financial forecasting typically involves these steps:

- Collect historical data: In forecasting, reliable and accurate data is everything. So, gather past sales data, expense records, and other relevant information to serve as the basis for the forecast.

- Set assumptions: Develop assumptions about factors such as market trends, customer growth, cost increases, and seasonality. These are the building blocks of a forecast.

- Create different scenarios: Create a base-case forecast, an optimistic forecast, and a pessimistic forecast. This helps the business understand how different situations will impact finances.

- Develop a financial model: Use tools like spreadsheets or forecasting software to create financial models that predict income, expenses, and profits.

- Review and update regularly: A forecast is not a one-time task; it should be reviewed and updated regularly based on the latest data and market conditions.

Here's a prompt you can use to ask for help with financial forecasting for their business:

Prompt:

Can you guide me through the financial forecasting process for my business? I'd like to understand how to:
- Collect and use historical data, like past sales and expenses, for accurate forecasting

- Set assumptions on market trends, customer growth, and costs

- Create different financial scenarios (base, optimistic, and pessimistic) to anticipate varied outcomes

- Develop a financial model to project income, expenses, and profits using tools like spreadsheets

- Regularly review and update the forecast based on current data and conditions

I'm looking to ensure financial viability and be prepared for different market situations.

Tools for Financial Forecasting

Today, a variety of tools are available to help businesses create financial forecasts, including:

- Excel or Google Sheets: Great for small businesses that need basic forecasting without a lot of bells and whistles.

- Forecasting software: Platforms like QuickBooks, Float, and PlanGuru provide more advanced forecasting features and integration with other financial data sources.

- CRM Integration: With platforms like HubSpot, integrating CRM data into forecasts can give insights into how customer leads and conversions will impact future revenue.

Budgeting for Business Success

Now, let's talk about the other aspect of financial planning: budgeting. In simpler terms, it's the process of creating a financial plan to track your income and expenses over a specific period. But it's much more than that. Budgeting isn't just about allocating money; it's about planning, controlling, and ensuring that your financial decisions are aligned with your business goals.

Without a budget, it's easy to spend more than your business can afford, especially in high-cost areas like marketing or inventory. With a budget, you and your team will have clear spending limits, which helps you focus on spending where it brings the most value.

Budgeting Process 101

Creating a budget doesn't have to be complicated. The best approach is to keep it simple. Here's a step-by-step guide to help small businesses get started with budgeting:

1. Set Your Goals

   Begin by setting financial goals for your business. These goals might include increasing sales by 20%, saving for an equipment purchase, or maintaining a certain level of profit. The budget should align with these goals to guide the overall direction of your spending.

2. Estimate Your Income

   The next step is to determine how much money you expect your business to make over a specific period—usually a month, quarter, or year.

3. Identify Fixed and Variable Costs

   To effectively budget, you need a clear understanding of your costs. Costs can generally be categorized as:

   ○ Fixed Costs: These are expenses that don't change significantly over time, such as rent, insurance, utilities, and salaries for permanent employees. These are the bills that must be paid regardless of how much revenue is coming in.

   ○ Variable Costs: These are costs that fluctuate depending on your level of business activity. They include raw materials, shipping, packaging, commissions, and marketing expenses. As your sales increase, your variable costs will also go up.

4. Create a Cash Flow Projection

Cash flow is the movement of money into and out of your business. A cash flow projection helps determine if you'll have enough cash on hand at any given point to cover your expenses.

5. Analyze Your Breakeven Point

Calculating your breakeven point—where total revenue equals total costs—helps determine how much you need to sell to cover all expenses. Understanding the breakeven point is vital for pricing products, planning promotions, and knowing when you're in profit territory.

6. Adjust and Rebalance

Once you've laid out income and expenses, compare them. If expenses are higher than income, you'll need to either cut unnecessary expenses or reconsider your priorities. Look for areas where you can cut costs without affecting the core operations of the business. Decide which expenses are most critical and consider deferring or reducing spending on less important items.

7. Monitor and Update the Budget Regularly

A budget isn't a static document—it should be revisited and updated regularly. Actual performance will inevitably differ from your initial estimates. By monitoring the budget, you can identify which costs exceeded expectations and which revenues were under or overestimated. Updating the budget allows for more accurate forecasting and better management.

Budgeting and Forecasting with AI

If you're a finance-averse person who dislikes crunching numbers, there's some good news. AI is here to lend a helping hand.

As already stated in the previous chapter, AI has rapidly become a game-changer in many aspects of business, like marketing and content creation. And with the latest advancement, you can use AI as an accountant, helping you with budgets and forecasting.

At the core, AI uses data and data analysis to uncover patterns that are too resource-intensive for humans. Humans can then inspect the patterns and make a more informed decision at a faster pace. In other words, With AI, decisions are based on data, not gut feelings. And this happens twice or thrice as fast.

AI Tools to Use for Budgeting and Forecasting

There are several AI tools that you can use to create budgets and forecast sales and revenue. Here are some tools I recommend:

- PlanGuru

PlanGuru is built for financial planning, budgeting, and forecasting with unlimited budgeting flexibility. Which means you can create a multi-department AI budget or forecast without restriction.

PlanGuru allows businesses to create detailed financial budgets by analyzing historical data and forecasts by simulating future scenarios. AI-powered insights help businesses spot trends and adjust their budgets accordingly.

- Jirav

Jirav is designed for small and mid-sized businesses to handle financial planning with AI-driven insights. One of the best features is it automates the budgeting process by integrating with existing data sources and creating dynamic budgets that adjust with real-time inputs.

- Xero

As a core accounting software, Xero uses AI and machine learning to analyze financial data and create budget templates based on historical data trends. It automatically updates budgets as financial transactions are logged, making it easy to keep budgets up to date.

- Vena Insights

Vena Insights is an AI-powered financial tool that integrates with existing systems to automate data collection, analysis, and reporting. Vena can pull in data from multiple sources, such as Excel, ERP, and CRM systems. With its AI-powered insights, Vena offers customized reports to monitor budget progress and performance.

- Domo

Domo is a cloud-based platform that offers business intelligence (BI) and data analytics with AI-powered insights. Designed for small and mid-sized businesses, it claims to increase revenue by almost $1 million through its AI-driven data analysis and reporting services.

Wrap Up

In this chapter, you learned the essential steps for making smart money moves to support your business. From exploring funding options to creating realistic financial forecasts, you now have a roadmap for managing finances strategically and securing the resources you need to grow.

Action Steps

1. Identify potential funding sources that best fit your business model.

2. Create a basic financial forecast for the next 12 months to guide spending and revenue goals.

3. Set up a process to monitor your finances regularly and make adjustments as needed.

Up Next

With funding and financial planning in place, you're ready to start thinking bigger. In the next chapter, we'll focus on scaling your business—covering strategies for expanding operations, reaching new markets, and optimizing processes to grow sustainably.

Chapter Six

Scaling to New Heights

O kay. So you're up and running and sales are coming in. There's some word-of-mouth among your first users and more people are lining up to learn more about your products and services. Perhaps you've hired an employee or two to carry out certain tasks, and life's great.

But here's a thing about business: your customer base doesn't remain the same. The people buying from you won't necessarily buy tomorrow. Some move on, others pass away. In other words, businesses always lose customers, regardless of how good their products are.

The only cure for it is to add new users and convert them into customers. This is often done through scaling. Scaling refers to the process of growing a business's operations and increasing its output or reach. It involves expanding existing operations, such as increasing production capacity, hiring more employees, or entering new markets.

Brian Rothenberg, a venture capitalist and a Partner at Defy.vc, while answering a question on why scaling is important for businesses, wrote, "Scaling is critical because sustainable growth tends to be the cure for everything else that can and does go wrong at a startup."

Scaling offers another crucial advantage: unlocking the full potential of your business. For example, if your startup is projected to generate $5 million in annual revenue, reaching that goal may require more than just sticking to your current approach. Scaling is the key to turning those projections into reality.

But there's a more lucrative and enticing reason why scaling a new business is so important.

More Time For Yourself

Why do we start a business? One reason is because of the urge to break free of the 9-to-5 grind and enjoy a lifestyle that grants more freedom and time. As most first-time entrepreneurs find out, they do break free from the 9-to-5 schedule, but only to get stuck in a 7-to-10 schedule. The business takes control of their lives turning into a nightmare and the dream slips away.

To regain control of your business, scaling is essential. By expanding your workforce, hiring or training capable leaders, and implementing efficient systems, you can delegate tasks and allow your business to run more independently. These leaders will help manage key operations and ensure systems run smoothly, reducing the need for your constant involvement. With strong leadership and streamlined processes in place, you'll be able to set clearer boundaries between work and personal life. This not only allows the business to thrive but also promotes a healthier work-life balance, giving you more quality time with family.

This chapter is all about how to scale your business to new heights. If you're stuck in sales, revenue, growth, or just day-to-day chores, it could mean that the time to scale and unlock the full potential has come.

In the next section, you'll learn about the steps startup founders take to scale their businesses and reach their goals.

What is Scaling a Business exactly?

Many business owners think scaling a business simply means increasing the headcount or expanding to new locations. While those are components of scaling a business, it's not the whole story. Therefore, let's start at the basics with a good definition of what it means to scale a business.

Scaling a business is like expanding a house. Just as you add more rooms to accommodate a growing family, you scale a business to handle increased demand, reach more customers, and generate higher revenue. But unlike building a house, scaling a business involves more than just physical expansion. It's about growing your operations in a way that maintains efficiency, profitability, and sustainability.

Take note of the three terms – efficiency, profitability, sustainability – because that's the end goal of a business scale-up.

Scaling can involve various aspects of your business, such as:

- Hiring more employees - As your business grows, you'll need additional staff to handle increased workload and responsibilities.

- Expanding your product or service offerings - Introducing new products or services can attract new customers and boost revenue.

- Entering new markets - Expanding your geographic reach can expose your business to new opportunities and customer bases.

- Improving your technology infrastructure - As your business grows, you may need to upgrade your technology systems to handle increased data and workload.

- Optimizing your operations - Streamlining processes and improving efficiency can help you scale your business more effectively.

Remember, scaling is not just about getting bigger; it's about growing sustainably and profitably. It requires careful planning, strategic decision-making, and a focus on maintaining quality and customer satisfaction. By understanding the principles of scaling, you can position your business for long-term success and growth.

Key Ingredients to a Successful Business Scale-Up

Scaling a business requires a few raw ingredients – just like baking a pizza. You combine the separate ingredients together to reach your end goals.

But just as different types of pizza call for different recipes, not every business requires the same ingredients for scaling up. For example, a corporation may require third-party financial audits before regulators approve the expansion. There's no such requirement for a small or midsize business. Therefore, the exact prerequisites to scaling a business vary.

That being said, there are some commonalities. Researchers have long been studying what businesses that scaled up successfully have in common. And based on the research, they have come up with frameworks. One such framework is the Six S framework proposed by Harvard Business School Professor Jeffrey Rayport.

Six S stands for:

Staff

Staff is the first element, emphasizing the importance of having the right people in place. As the business grows, it's crucial to hire talented individuals who fit the company's vision. These employees should be trained and developed to take on more responsibilities as the company expands. Strong leadership is also essential to manage the growing team and oversee daily operations.

Shared Values

Shared values refer to the company's culture and core principles. These values guide decision-making and behavior. As the business scales, maintaining a consistent culture ensures that everyone in the company, including new hires, is aligned with the company's mission. This consistency is important for both internal operations and customer relations.

Structure

The third S is about your business structure and making adjustments in a way that supports growth. Clear roles, responsibilities, and processes allow the business to function smoothly as it grows. Standardizing key processes helps maintain quality and efficiency, even with a larger team. However, it's also important to keep the structure flexible so the company can adapt to new challenges.

Speed

Speed focuses on the company's ability to act quickly. Businesses that scale successfully are agile in decision-making and execution. Streamlining operations and removing unnecessary steps can increase speed and efficiency. Using technology and automation to handle routine tasks can also help the company respond faster to customer needs.

Scope

Scope refers to expanding the company's reach. This might mean offering new products or services, entering new markets, or targeting different customer segments. Increasing the scope of the business helps diversify revenue streams and reduce reliance on a single market or product.

Series X

Finally, Series X focuses on financial resources. Whether through investment rounds or reinvesting profits, having enough capital is critical for scaling a business. This allows the company to invest in marketing, hire more staff, and expand its operations, among other things. In addition to funding, forming partnerships and alliances can provide resources and expertise to help the business grow.

The Six S framework ensures that all aspects of the business are working together during the scaling process. By focusing on these six areas, companies can grow effectively while maintaining stability and alignment.

As previously mentioned, the Six S framework is just one way of looking at the components of scaling a business. There are alternate models as well. As an example, here's a more simplified model that you can use to determine whether your business is ready to scale:

Product-Market Fit

Arguably, the most important requisite to scaling is product-market fit. It's like ensuring your house is built in a location where people want to live. Otherwise, you'll be building a house in an inhabitable environment. Before scaling, conduct market research to understand your target audience's needs and preferences.

A Solid Business Model

A business model is the blueprint for your business. It outlines your value proposition, revenue streams, and cost structure. A well-defined business model provides a clear roadmap for growth. Identify multiple revenue streams to reduce your reliance on a single source of income. Analyze your costs and find ways to reduce expenses or improve efficiency.

Lead Acquisition and Nurturing System

Scaling involves generating consistent sales, preferably at a lower cost. Develop a comprehensive marketing strategy to attract and generate qualified leads. Create a well-defined sales funnel to guide leads through the customer journey and convert them into customers. Use a CRM system to track leads, manage interactions, and analyze sales performance.

A Strong Leadership and Team

Right people are crucial for driving growth. A visionary leader can inspire and motivate employees to achieve common goals. Foster a positive and collaborative work culture where employees feel valued and empowered. Invest in employee training and development to ensure your team has the skills and knowledge to support scaling.

Proper Finance

Money is essential for sustainable growth. Maintain accurate financial records, create budgets, and track your financial performance. Secure adequate funding to support growth initiatives. Develop financial projections to anticipate future needs and make informed decisions about resource allocation.

Partnerships and Alliances

Partnering with non-competing businesses can help you expand your reach, access new markets, or leverage complementary resources. You can also consider joint ventures to share risks and rewards. Build strong relationships with suppliers to ensure a reliable supply of goods or services.

Besides the ones discussed above, there may be other prerequisites to scaling a business. Thus, understand your business at the basic level and ensure you have them covered prior to scaling.

Scaling Any Business in 10 Steps

With the theoretical knowledge, now let's proceed towards practical work. Once you've established a business and gained traction, it's time to scale.

As with anything, it's important not to complicate matters and keep things simple. With a focus on simplicity, here are the 10 steps to successfully scaling a business:

1. Establish product-market fit

2. Develop a scalable business model

3. Secure funding

4. Build a lead generation and nurturing system

5. Streamline operations

6. Build a strong team

7. Consider outsourcing

8. Leverage technology

9. Expand market reach

10. Monitor key metrics

Establish Product-Market Fit

If you're at the scalability stage of business, chances are high that you've found product-market fit. If not, you should seriously reconsider the decision to scale. Without this alignment, scaling efforts are likely to fail because there won't be enough demand to sustain growth.

Achieving product-market fit involves deeply understanding your customers' needs, refining your offerings, and testing how well your product resonates in the market.

Some areas where you should get clarity are:

- Ideal customers

- Ensuring minimum viable profit (MVP) resonates with the customers

- Profit margin

Dropbox is a well-known example of a company that achieved product-market fit before scaling. When Dropbox first launched, the company didn't invest heavily in marketing or growth. Instead, it focused on creating a minimum viable product—a simple file-sharing service that solved a real problem: the difficulty of sharing files across different devices.

Develop a Scalable Business Model

Successful scaling requires a business model that can support rapid growth. Therefore, you need to develop a scalable business model.

A scalable business model is one that can grow and handle increased demand without a corresponding rise in costs. Developing this model ensures that as your customer base grows, your expenses don't grow at the same rate.

A good example of it is King Digital Entertainment, the creators of Candy Crush Saga. The company scaled the game from mid-2012 to mid-2013. During this timeframe, its revenue increased by 12-fold while cost increased only by 6-fold. This ensured the game remained profitable after the scale.

When developing a scalable business model, focus on these things:

- Unit economics

- Revenue streams

- Fixed and variable costs

- Cost per customer acquisition

With a profitable model in place, you ensure scaling operations won't burn cash faster than your revenue growth..

Secure Funding

Scaling a business isn't without cost. Depending on the business size and scope of scale, you're likely to see a significant rise in expenses. To make this happen, ensure you have sufficient funding.

As your business grows, so do the financial demands, whether it's for hiring staff, expanding marketing efforts, developing new products, or entering new markets. Having adequate funding ensures that you have the resources to scale without sacrificing quality.

Start by calculating how much capital is required to scale. This involves looking at your current financial situation and forecasting future expenses related to growth. Consider costs such as:

- Hiring additional staff

- Increasing inventory

- Expanding marketing efforts

- Upgrading infrastructure (e.g., technology, office space)

- Developing new products or services

Break down these expenses over a set timeline to determine how much capital you need at each stage of scaling. This will help you avoid raising too little or too much (which could dilute your ownership unnecessarily).

Build a Lead Generation and Nurturing System

To scale a business, having a consistent way to generate and nurture leads is essential. A lead generation system focuses on attracting potential customers to your business. In contrast, a lead nurturing system engages and guides those leads through your sales funnel until they become paying customers. Together, these systems ensure a steady flow of prospects, fueling growth.

For this, you may have to tweak your marketing and spend more money on advertising. But it's not the only way. When Hotmail wanted to scale operations, it included the following message on every mail that was sent via Hotmail:

```
PS: I love you.Get your
free e-mail at Hotmail
```

Within 1.5 years, it grew to 12 million users, literally for free. Later, Hotmail was acquired by Microsoft for a sweet $400 million.

So, get creative with your lead gen system and try different tactics.

Streamline Operations

When you scale, you need to ensure there are as few bottlenecks as possible. Otherwise, this will reduce the speed at which your business can scale. This is done through streamlining operations.

Streamlining operations means refining your internal processes, reducing inefficiencies, and automating repetitive tasks. This is done across the board, from marketing to production to HR to finance. If you're a one-person company, streamlining operations means automating as much as possible.

Start by conducting a thorough review of your existing operations. Break down each function of your business, from production to customer service, and identify areas where time, money, or resources are being wasted. Then take steps to optimize or eliminate the inefficiencies.

Build a Strong Team

As a company grows, it becomes much more about its people than the products and services. A strong, motivated, and capable team can help you innovate, adapt to challenges, and handle increased demand. As your business scales, hiring and developing a team with the right balance of skills and leadership potential is essential.

When hiring, look for candidates who not only have the technical skills required for the job but also resonate with your company's vision and mission. Zappos, the online shoe retailer, is famous for hiring employees based on cultural fit. They emphasize aligning new hires with the company's core values. Zappos even offers employees money to quit during the onboarding process if they feel they're not a good fit. This approach ensures that only those committed to the company's culture stay and thrive.

Consider Outsourcing

Employees are not the only way to get things done. The other method is outsourcing. Outsourcing – the act of delegating tasks to an outside firm or freelancers – can be a key strategy when scaling your business. It allows you to access specialized skills, reduce overhead costs, and focus on core activities that drive growth.

Determine what parts of your business are most valuable to keep in-house—typically functions related directly to your product or service. You can outsource tasks that take up time and resources but don't directly contribute to your company's growth. Think of accounting if you're in a bakery business.

Leverage Technology

Technology has changed the way businesses scale. On a positive note, it has made scaling faster. The impact of technology on business scaling is so deep that investors have started distinguishing between a scalable and non-scalable business based on how tech-savvy a business is. Generally, a tech-heavy business is considered more scalable than a company that relies on physical stuff.

In scaling, you should keep technology at the core. Implement technology in every operation of the business, whether it is project management, sales, marketing, customer service, or delivery. By leveraging technology, you can automate processes, increase efficiency, and improve customer experience, all of which are essential for managing growth.

Expand Market Reach

Scaling requires that you broaden your offerings and tap into new segments, geographic regions, or product categories to increase your customer base and grow revenue.

Tesla initially targeted the luxury electric car market with its flagship Tesla Roadster but expanded its reach by developing more affordable models, such as the Model 3, to attract a broader customer base. This strategic move enabled Tesla to expand into new market segments and significantly increase its customer base. Today Tesla is among the most valuable companies.

To apply this strategy, identify areas where you can expand and roll out products and capitalize on those opportunities.

Monitor Key Metrics

The final step to scaling a business is setting up and monitoring key metrics. These help you determine whether you're on the right path or need to pivot to a new strategy.

Before you begin scaling, you need to determine the key performance indicators (KPIs) that are most important to your business. These metrics should be aligned with your business goals and growth objectives. Financial KPIs such as revenue growth, profit margins, and cash flow are critical for all businesses. However, other metrics, such as customer acquisition cost (CAC), customer lifetime value (CLV), and churn rate, can be equally important for evaluating how efficiently your business is scaling.

Wrap Up

This chapter guided you through the process of scaling your business strategically. You learned how to assess your current capacity, streamline operations, and enter new markets without losing quality or focus. Scaling effectively requires both careful planning and bold moves.

Action Steps

1. Review your operations and identify key areas where efficiency can be improved.

2. Set specific growth goals and timelines, such as expanding to a new market or increasing production capacity.

3. Build a support system—whether through hiring, partnerships, or outsourcing—to manage increased demands.

Up Next

In the next chapter, we'll dive into the strategies for seizing new markets. You'll discover how to analyze market opportunities, tailor your approach, and position your brand to make a strong impact in unfamiliar territories.

In retail, for example, your team has been with you for years, and they've become experts in handling day-to-day operations. They're even taking the lead on new initiatives, like suggesting ways to improve customer service or streamline inventory management. When your team is ready to step up, you have the support system in place for expansion.

Inability to meet customer demand

Many times business owners think you need to expand when sales are plateauing. But the best expansion happens when your sales are exploding. Not being able to meet demand means you're leaving money on the table. And to capture those customers, you should expand your operations.

Let's say you run a busy hair salon. You're booked solid for weeks, and you can't fit in new clients. You're turning away business because you don't have enough chairs or stylists. This is a clear sign that you've outgrown your current setup, and it's time to think about hiring more staff or opening a second location.

Your customers demand more

The best signals come right from your customers. After all, the customer is always right.

If your users come up to you with requests for more features or services, you should know you've hit the "expansion" jackpot.

Top companies leverage customer feedback as a powerful tool to drive product innovation and enhance user experience. Take the example of Netflix. It initially started as an online DVD rental company. User feedback led to the introduction of features like personalized recommendations, offline viewing, and multiple profiles.

You need requests like these to know you need to expand.

You've built a strong brand and reputation

When your business has a solid reputation and loyal customer base, expansion becomes less risky. Positive reviews, word-of-mouth referrals, and repeat customers are all signs that your brand is ready to grow.

Without the reputation, you'll have a hard time convincing new customers and likely experience longer sales cycles. This is considered inefficient and cost-intensive. Thus, ensure trust is in place among your existing users.

You've identified a market opportunity

Ben Horowitz, the celebrated venture capitalist, once said, "Markets that don't exist don't care how smart you are." And you should keep that in mind when expanding.

If you've identified an underserved market or see a new trend emerging that fits your business, it's worth exploring expansion to capture that opportunity.

For example, a fitness studio owner may notice that there's growing interest in virtual workout classes. While they may have traditionally only offered in-person classes, expanding into the virtual space could allow them to tap into a whole new market—people who prefer to work out from home.

You feel ready for new challenges

Sometimes, it's about you, the business owner. If you feel comfortable in your current operations but crave a new challenge or see more potential for your business, it might be time to scale up.

Backed with data and information, you should take up the challenge and expand your other market opportunities.

However, be wary of Shiny Object Syndrome. Shiny Object Syndrome (SOS) is the constant pull to chase after every new opportunity or trend that seems exciting, without fully thinking about whether it's the right fit for your goals. It's like being distracted by the next "shiny object" that catches your attention, often at the cost of what's already working or what truly matters.

You're meeting your metrics

The US Chamber of Commerce is the world's largest business federation, with more than 3 million members. It advises both new and expert business owners on trends and tactics.

In one of the blog posts titled "6 signs your company is ready to expand" it lists "you're meeting your metrics" as the number 1 sign. And I strongly agree with that.

You should only be expanding into new markets if your KPI or key performance indicators say so. It's a data-driven way to expand your business rather than solely on gut and instincts. And time and again, it is seen that data-based businesses have a higher chance of success.

The exact metrics you'd track are specific to the business. But generally, you'd want:

- Cost and expenses

- Profit margin

- Cash flow

- Customer acquisition cost

- Customer lifetime value

- Churn rate

- Inventory turnover

- Market penetration

You have a solid team of employees

Expansion requires a team that can handle more responsibility. If your staff is well-trained, reliable, and eager for new challenges, that's a strong indicator that your business can grow without falling apart.

Chapter Seven

Seizing New Market Opportunities

I n the previous chapter, I taught you how and when to scale a business. To reiterate, scaling is the only way to maximize your business potential and make the biggest impact in the world.

Here, we're going to niche down and focus on something specific: finding new market opportunities.

Finding new opportunities is one way of scaling a business. And in some cases, it's the best one. There are times when growth seems elusive in one market segment. INSEAD business theorists Renée Mauborgne and W. Chan Kim call these segments "Red Oceans." In those cases, the best way to achieve growth and scale is by seizing new market opportunities.

But as is most things with running a business, it's easier said than done. But with proven strategies, the right information, and lady luck, you can find winning markets and capitalize on them.

When to Find New Markets

The thought of expanding into new markets is tempting. But it's important to time your jump. Jump too soon or too late, and you may miss the mark.

Fortunately, there's a way to know if it's ripe to expand into new markets. You need to look for certain signs. If they're green, you're good to go. Let's have a look at those signals.

In retail, for example, your team has been with you for years, and they've become experts in handling day-to-day operations. They're even taking the lead on new initiatives, like suggesting ways to improve customer service or streamline inventory management. When your team is ready to step up, you have the support system in place for expansion.

Inability to meet customer demand

Many times business owners think you need to expand when sales are plateauing. But the best expansion happens when your sales are exploding. Not being able to meet demand means you're leaving money on the table. And to capture those customers, you should expand your operations.

Let's say you run a busy hair salon. You're booked solid for weeks, and you can't fit in new clients. You're turning away business because you don't have enough chairs or stylists. This is a clear sign that you've outgrown your current setup, and it's time to think about hiring more staff or opening a second location.

Your customers demand more

The best signals come right from your customers. After all, the customer is always right.

If your users come up to you with requests for more features or services, you should know you've hit the "expansion" jackpot.

Top companies leverage customer feedback as a powerful tool to drive product innovation and enhance user experience. Take the example of Netflix. It initially started as an online DVD rental company. User feedback led to the introduction of features like personalized recommendations, offline viewing, and multiple profiles.

You need requests like these to know you need to expand.

You've built a strong brand and reputation

When your business has a solid reputation and loyal customer base, expansion becomes less risky. Positive reviews, word-of-mouth referrals, and repeat customers are all signs that your brand is ready to grow.

Without the reputation, you'll have a hard time convincing new customers and likely experience longer sales cycles. This is considered inefficient and cost-intensive. Thus, ensure trust is in place among your existing users.

You've identified a market opportunity

Ben Horowitz, the celebrated venture capitalist, once said, "Markets that don't exist don't care how smart you are." And you should keep that in mind when expanding.

If you've identified an underserved market or see a new trend emerging that fits your business, it's worth exploring expansion to capture that opportunity.

For example, a fitness studio owner may notice that there's growing interest in virtual workout classes. While they may have traditionally only offered in-person classes, expanding into the virtual space could allow them to tap into a whole new market—people who prefer to work out from home.

You feel ready for new challenges

Sometimes, it's about you, the business owner. If you feel comfortable in your current operations but crave a new challenge or see more potential for your business, it might be time to scale up.

Backed with data and information, you should take up the challenge and expand your other market opportunities.

However, be wary of Shiny Object Syndrome. Shiny Object Syndrome (SOS) is the constant pull to chase after every new opportunity or trend that seems exciting, without fully thinking about whether it's the right fit for your goals. It's like being distracted by the next "shiny object" that catches your attention, often at the cost of what's already working or what truly matters.

In business, this means jumping from one idea, tool, or project to the next, lured by the promise of quick success or instant rewards. The problem? You spread yourself too thin, leaving important tasks unfinished and missing out on the deeper progress that comes from staying focused and committed.

While innovation is key to growth, Shiny Object Syndrome can lead to wasted resources—time, energy, and money—on things that might not be the best move for your business in the long run. It prevents you from honing in on what truly drives success, leaving you with a lot of half-finished projects and no clear direction.

Market Research: The Secret Weapon for Seizing New Opportunities

Growing up, I always admired superheroes (I'm sure you do too). I was in awe of the web-shooters of Spiderman and Superman's immense power. Soon I realized that it's their powers that make them special. It's what enables them to do magical things.

Likewise, when you take up the task of seizing new market opportunities, you need your own secret weapons. And that is market research.

In today's fast-changing world, customer preferences, industry trends, and market dynamics are always shifting. By consistently gathering and analyzing data, businesses can make informed decisions about when, where, and how to expand.

More specifically, there are good reasons why businesses widely adopt continuous market research.

Staying ahead of customer needs

One of the most significant benefits of ongoing market research is the ability to stay ahead of customer needs. Consumer expectations are constantly evolving. What worked a year ago may no longer be relevant today.

For instance, according to a report by PwC, 73% of customers say that experience is a key factor in their purchasing decisions. This shift in consumer behavior highlights the importance of businesses keeping track of what their customers want in real-time. By doing so, they can ensure their expansion plans align with current market demands.

Spotting emerging trends early

Continuous research also helps businesses identify and respond to emerging trends. Market trends, particularly technological advancements, can create opportunities or challenges for businesses. Companies that fail to adapt often fall behind their competitors. A good example is the rise of e-commerce.

In 2023, global e-commerce sales accounted for over 19% of total retail sales, according to Statista. Companies that were quick to recognize this shift and invested in online shopping infrastructure gained a competitive edge. On the other hand, businesses that hesitated lost out on substantial market share. Regular market research helps companies spot these trends early and adjust their strategies accordingly.

Mitigating risk in new markets

Expanding a business is always a risk. There are uncertainties about new markets, customer behavior, and local competition. Continuous market research can help businesses mitigate these risks by providing valuable insights into market potential, competitive landscapes, and customer expectations in new areas.

For example, if a restaurant chain is considering opening new locations in a different city, market research can reveal local food preferences, spending habits, and competitors. With this information, the chain can tailor its menu and marketing efforts to meet the needs of the new customer base, reducing the likelihood of failure.

Efficient resource allocation

Market research also plays a vital role in helping businesses allocate resources effectively. Expansion requires investment in areas such as marketing, staffing, and infrastructure. Without proper data, businesses may spend resources inefficiently.

According to a report by the Harvard Business Review, companies that rely on data-driven decision-making are 5% more productive and 6% more profitable than their competitors. By continually gathering market data, businesses can make informed choices about where to allocate funds, ensuring that they get the best possible return on their investments.

Staying competitive

Finally, continuous market research helps businesses maintain a competitive edge during expansion. Competitors are always looking for ways to capture more market share. By conducting regular research, businesses can monitor their competition's strategies and adjust their own accordingly. This proactive approach allows companies to stay competitive and seize opportunities before their rivals do.

Continuous Market Research Methodology

The global market research sector is a significant industry, generating billions of dollars in revenue annually. While exact figures can vary, it's estimated to be worth well over $80 billion.

Market research companies provide valuable insights into consumer behavior, market trends, and industry dynamics. The people working in this sector drive major business decisions across the world through their research and findings.

They spend years honing their skills. But fortunately, people like you and me don't have to. You can use their techniques to carry out continuous market research to seize new opportunities. Below are some of the core techniques used by researchers to evaluate and understand their markets.

Surveys

Ever received a "Take a quick survey" email from your favorite brand? That's continuous market research in action.

Surveys are arguably the most commonly used method in market research. They provide businesses with direct feedback from customers and help identify trends in consumer behavior. Companies use online, phone, or in-person surveys to collect data about customer preferences, product satisfaction, and purchasing habits.

Imagine a coffee shop chain that wants to expand into a new city. The company sends out a survey asking potential customers about their coffee preferences, how often they visit cafes, and which locations are most convenient. By analyzing the responses, the business can tailor its offerings to the preferences of the new market before opening its doors.

Focus groups

The second most common method is focus groups, which involve gathering a small group of people to discuss a product, service, or concept in depth. Businesses can gain rich, qualitative data by observing how participants react and interact with each other's opinions. Focus groups provide insights that numbers alone can't, such as emotional responses and personal motivations.

The main concern with focus groups is they tend to be expensive. It takes effort to sort out the best candidates for focus group sessions, agree on a common time, and reward them for their efforts. However, with a bit of strategy, you can complete a focus session without spending much.

All you need is past customer data, sort out the best candidates for an interview, and set up a Zoom session. As a reward, you can gift them a discount or priority access to upcoming products.

Qualitative interviews

Along with focus sessions, qualitative interviews with a single person work best. This is where you sit down with a single person and talk like you would at a coffee shop with a friend.

One-on-one interviews allow businesses to dive deep into the customer experience. This method involves detailed conversations that help understand a customer's motivations, desires, and frustrations. It provides more in-depth insight than surveys and can uncover pain points that weren't previously considered.

Social media listening

Social media is more than a place where you update your status. It's a goldmine for businesses looking for insights into their customers. And there are dedicated apps that enable you to do that. This is called social media listening.

Social media listening involves tracking and analyzing online conversations about a brand, product, or industry. Platforms like Twitter, Instagram, and Facebook allow businesses to gauge public sentiment, spot emerging trends, and even respond to customer concerns in real-time.

A fashion brand like H&M uses social media listening to track customer reactions to new collections. If they notice customers frequently discussing a particular style or trend, they adjust their inventory or marketing strategy to capitalize on what's trending, ensuring they remain relevant and on-trend.

Observations

Observational research involves watching customers interact with a product or service in a real-world setting. This method helps businesses see what customers do, rather than relying on what they say they do, providing insights that might not come out through direct questioning.

Grocery stores often use observational research by watching how customers navigate the aisles. They might observe that customers spend more time browsing organic products.

This insight can prompt them to expand their organic offerings or reposition these products for better visibility, improving sales.

Field trials

Field trials involve testing a product or service in a small, controlled environment before fully launching it. This method is especially useful for expansion because it allows businesses to assess the real-world impact of their product or service without committing too many resources.

A fast-food chain might test a new menu item in a few select locations before rolling it out nationwide. If the new item sells well and customer feedback is positive, the chain can confidently introduce it in more locations. On the other hand, if the item doesn't perform as expected, they can modify the recipe or marketing before investing heavily in it.

Competitive analysis

Continuous market research includes keeping a close eye on competitors. Businesses can analyze what their competitors are doing—whether it's new product launches, pricing strategies, or marketing tactics—and use this information to inform their own strategies.

A good example of a competitive analysis is Netflix. Netflix closely watches competitors like Disney+ and Amazon Prime to see how they price their services, what content is trending, and how customers respond. By analyzing competitors' actions, Netflix can adjust its own strategies, such as focusing on original content or tweaking subscription tiers to stay competitive in the streaming market.

Public data

Public data from government reports, industry studies, or trade associations provides valuable insights that can inform expansion decisions. The best part is this data is often freely available and can reveal trends in demographics, spending habits and broader economic conditions.

A real estate company might use census data to determine population growth in different areas. If the data shows a particular city is growing rapidly and has a high number of young professionals, the company might target that area for new property developments.

Purchased data

In some cases, businesses purchase data from third-party providers like Adobe and Nielsen. In most cases, these are the market research organizations that gather and compile data. This method is particularly useful for gathering insights that are difficult or time-consuming to collect independently. Purchased data often includes detailed consumer profiles, spending habits, and industry-specific reports.

While the reports tend to be expensive, they are often reliable and worth the investment, especially as you're entering new markets.

Sales data analysis

You might be sitting on a pile of rich information without even knowing. The sales figures that you've got saved on Excel sheets or CRM can offer valuation information on future growth prospects.

Analyzing past sales performance helps companies spot trends, identify popular products, and understand seasonal patterns. It also reveals areas where improvements can be made, such as reducing inventory costs or adjusting pricing strategies.

Amazon uses its massive sales data to recommend products to customers based on their past purchases. The company's ability to analyze millions of transactions helps it identify customer preferences, seasonal trends, and successful products, guiding future decisions on inventory management and marketing strategies.

The most successful companies use a mix of methods to gauge market opportunities. You should prioritize the ones that are within your comfort level and budget.

Identifying and Capitalizing on New Market Opportunities

Finding new opportunities starts with identifying them. Your entrepreneurial eyes perhaps find opportunities at every nook and corner of the street. But it's not worth, nor feasible, to chase every moment. Thankfully, there are a few ways that help you spot the feasible ones.

Not all that glitters is gold

Business owners and investors alike are always on the hunt for the so-called "Next big thing." From flying cars to quantum computers to anti-aging technology, you can find them everywhere.

But smart investors know something that others don't (or perhaps ignore on purpose): not all that glitters is gold.

The latest example is crypto and NFT or non-fungible tokens. While Bitcoin and other cryptocurrencies are still around, the world-changing potential they once claimed is all but gone. And as it turned out, NFT collectibles were nothing but another digital gold rush.

As a responsible business owner, you should always be skeptical of overhyped trends and fads that do not bring any business value, especially in the long run.

Just because NFT collectibles are in the news doesn't mean you should expand into it. You are free to experiment, but considerable investment is always a big no.

Conduct a gap analysis

In any industry there exist certain gaps that existing players are not meeting. And by carefully analyzing and identifying, you can expand into these gaps to grow your business.

Identifying gaps in the market involves looking for unmet needs or underserved customer segments. Gaps might include product features that customers desire, but competitors don't offer or geographic regions where there's little competition. Look for inefficiencies in your industry and find ways to fill those voids.

Monitor industry and consumer trends

Our world rarely stays the same. New inventions, tech, ideas, and customer choice alter how things are done. This invariably creates new market and consumer trends.

For example, the surge in remote work created an increased demand for virtual collaboration. Businesses like Zoom and Slack fulfilled this market need and became unicorns. Other companies, too, adapted to the growing trend by offering related products, such as office supplies for home setups, contactless delivery, etc.

By understanding emerging trends, you can identify new market segments that align with your offerings.

Monitor related industries

Many business executives make the mistake of overtly scrutinizing their own industry for growth and expansion opportunities. But research shows that at times, the best opportunities come from outside your industry.

This is evident from the fact that four in ten companies look outside of their domain for new ideas. This is because developments in one sector can create demand in another. For instance, the growth of e-commerce has fueled demand for logistics services, packaging, and online marketing tools.

Thus, keep tabs on industries that are adjacent to your own. Look for innovations, customer needs, or new technologies that could influence your market and identify opportunities in the same.

Keep an eye on the political landscape

The political environment plays a significant role in shaping business opportunities. Changes in regulations, tax policies, and trade agreements can open up new markets or create barriers in existing ones.

When the European Union imposed stricter regulations on data privacy (GDPR), players that were quick to adapt gained a competitive advantage. Many businesses also offered GDPR-complaint services and saw immediate success.

By staying informed about political developments, businesses can either mitigate risks or leverage new opportunities.

Low-end market opportunities

There's a theory in business that goes like, "Incumbent players always try for the highest margin segments of a market and underserve low margin segments. New players can exploit the low-end market opportunities without drawing the ire of incumbents who don't fight back due to lower margins."

This theory is called the low-end market opportunity theory by Clayton Christensen. Using this theory, you can analyze existing industries and find low-end opportunities for expansion. And you won't have to fight the existing players as well, thereby keeping the costs down.

Using ChatGPT To Find New Market Opportunities

There are specialized AI tools that you can use to find new opportunities in the market. But the simplest of them all is ChatGPT. ChatGPT is trained on a massive dataset of text, enabling it to analyze patterns, trends, and emerging opportunities within your industry. By feeding it with relevant data, you can gain valuable insights into consumer behavior, market trends, and competitor activities.

ChatGPT can help you spot underserved niches or unmet needs in the market. By analyzing customer feedback, social media conversations, and industry reports, it can identify gaps where your business can differentiate itself and offer unique solutions.

You can begin with a simple prompt like this, "I operate in the [niche] in [location]. I want to expand my business. Help me find new and related opportunities based on the latest data. Make use of the internet to find the latest information."

In this case, you're directing ChatGPT to search for new information, which requires a paid version at this time.

Alternatively, you can feed data to ChatGPT via attachments. Use your original market research and the latest market trends and ask ChatGPT to find relevant opportunities for you. "I've attached my original market research and a business report on the latest trends. I operate in [niche] and want to expand. Find relevant opportunities for me."

With few iterations, you should figure out the right unmet needs in an industry with AI.

Wrap Up

This chapter explored strategies for breaking into new markets. From conducting market research to positioning your brand effectively, you're now equipped to take confident steps into new areas, attracting a fresh audience and expanding your reach.

Action Steps

1. Research potential new markets and identify the ones with the most promise.

2. Tailor your marketing and sales approach to resonate with this new audience.

3. Set clear goals and timelines for entering and growing in these markets.

Up Next

In the final chapter, we'll look to the future of business with AI. You'll learn how to integrate AI into your operations, from enhancing customer experiences to streamlining internal processes, and prepare your business to stay competitive in the age of technology.

Chapter Eight

The Future with AI

In the previous chapter, under the "How to identify and capitalize on new market opportunities" section, I cautioned against the latest trends that are sold as "gold." Not all that glitters is gold.

Many people put AI in the same glittery bracket. They claim AI is nothing but a new concept sold by greedy Silicon Valley venture capitalists. While some criticism and a healthy dose of skepticism is valid, AI is something that cannot be unseen.

Artificial Intelligence (AI) is everywhere. Whether you're running a local coffee shop or managing a growing e-commerce store, AI is starting to shape how we do business in ways that were hard to imagine just a few years ago. For small and mid-sized business owners, it can seem like AI is something reserved for big companies with huge tech budgets, but that's not the case anymore.

I remember when I first started hearing about AI. Like many, I thought it was something out of a science fiction movie—futuristic robots and machines doing all the work. But then, I started seeing it pop up in real-world situations. Take email marketing, for example. My friend, who owns a small online retail store, used to spend hours figuring out the best time to send emails to her customers. Then, she discovered an AI-powered tool that did it all for her. Not only did it save her time, but it also boosted her sales by sending personalized recommendations based on customer behavior. She couldn't believe how simple it was, and neither could I.

Since then, I have taken an increased interest in AI and the latest developments. And I've distilled my acquired knowledge in this chapter.

Here, you'll learn about the future of AI, how to distinguish between AI hype and reality and how to use AI for your business. We have already covered a whole lot of the business applications of AI tools, from content creation to market research. In the sections below, we expand on them.

AI: Hype vs Reality

When it comes to AI, it's easy to get caught up in the media buzz. Headlines boast about how AI will revolutionize everything from healthcare to retail, and you've probably heard talk about how AI will either solve all our problems or take over our jobs.

The truth, however, lies somewhere in between. AI has immense potential, but there's also a lot of hype that can cloud its real value for businesses, especially for small and mid-sized ones. The top dogs have the budget to experiment with AI, lose money, and still be profitable.

So, the big question is how to differentiate between AI hype and reality. There's no proven system or methodology. But you can get to the truth by answering a few fundamental questions.

- Does it solve a real problem? AI should address a specific need within your business, like reducing manual labor, improving customer service, or increasing sales.

- Is it proven? Look for AI tools that have demonstrated success in similar businesses or industries.

- How does this AI compare to human performance on the same task? The primary benefit of AI is it does tasks faster than a human. Thus, compare the results and the time taken.

- Can you scale it? AI solutions should grow with your business, offering room for expansion without the need for constant updates or a tech expert on staff.

- What are the potential risks and challenges associated with this AI? AI systems often collect and analyze vast amounts of personal data, raising privacy concerns. Thus, inspect potential drawbacks.

AI expert Andrew Ng, one of the pioneers of machine learning, once said, "AI is the new electricity." What he means is that AI, like electricity, will soon be woven into the fabric of everyday business, powering systems in the background without us even noticing.

This grounded perspective highlights AI's potential to improve the way businesses run, but it also suggests that AI's value comes from its usefulness, not its flashiness.

Emerging Trends in AI For Businesses

Ever since ChatGPT was released to the public, AI has captivated both the public and organizational imagination. The collective interest in AI technology has increased since.

So, let's dive deeper into the latest AI trend and explore some real-world applications that demonstrate how AI is delivering tangible results for businesses of all sizes.

GenAI

Generative AI refers to AI systems that can create new content with simple inputs. Unlike traditional AI, which primarily analyzes or recognizes existing data, generative AI is capable of producing novel outputs. These systems are often based on advanced machine learning techniques, particularly Generative Adversarial Networks (GANs) or large-scale transformer models like GPT, which is used by OpenAI, the creator of ChatGPT.

Tools like ChatGPT or Jasper AI are already being used by businesses to automate the creation of blog posts, social media updates, email campaigns, and more. GenAI can produce draft content that human writers can refine, dramatically speeding up content production.

In the coming years, GenAI is poised to influence many more aspects of businesses.

Multimodal Machine Learning

Multimodal machine learning refers to AI models that can process and understand multiple types of data simultaneously, such as text, images, video, and audio. This means you can upload an audio sample and ask AI to create a document with text input. How cool is that?

Multimodal machine learning uses several neural networks to process different types of data streams and then combines the insights from each. For instance, an AI system could analyze a video by interpreting both the visual content and the spoken words within that video to understand its full context.

YouTube uses multimodal AI to recommend videos by analyzing both the visual content (thumbnails) and the video descriptions and tags. This ensures more personalized recommendations by understanding both what is shown in the video and how it is described. This opens up a new era in how tech works.

AI-Powered Automation

AI will have the most impact on automation. Redundant, manual processes that do not involve creative thinking will eventually be automated with AI.

Today, Robotic Process Automation (RPA) tools like UiPath or Blue Prism can handle repetitive tasks such as invoicing, payroll, and order processing with minimal human intervention.

Accounting software like Xero uses AI to automatically categorize transactions, match invoices, and generate financial reports. This reduces the need for manual data entry, freeing up accountants to focus on more complex tasks like financial planning.

Automation is also being widely adopted in marketing. Once you sign up for a newsletter, you get a steady stream of emails. These are automatically set in email automation tools like HubSpot and MailChimp.

AI Assistant

In a blog post, Bill Gates predicted that everyone who is online will have an AI-powered assistant working for them. He said, "In the near future, anyone who's online will be able to have a personal assistant powered by artificial intelligence that's far beyond today's technology." He predicted the timeline for the next five years (starting from 2023).

On his prophecy, he added, "Agents are smarter. They're proactive- capable of making suggestions before you ask for them."

This voice is echoed by the NVIDIA CEO, who on the NVIDIA blog said, "Every single company, every single job within the company, will have AI assistance."

With billions of dollars being poured into the development of AI assistants, it only makes sense to follow the trend and keep pace with it.

AI-Powered Customer Support

Just like users will have AI-powered assistants, businesses will have to equip themselves with an army of AI assistants to handle their customers.

AI-driven support systems typically use a combination of chatbots, voice assistants, and algorithms to process customer inquiries. These systems can analyze customer messages or queries in real time and respond appropriately by pulling information from a database of pre-programmed responses or learning from past interactions.

Some AI systems are also self-learning, meaning they get smarter over time by analyzing customer interactions.

A major benefit of AI in customer support is its 24/7 availability, helping customers at any time. AI chatbots and voice assistants can handle customer queries outside of regular business hours, ensuring customers get the help they need whenever they need it.

As this saves huge time and money for businesses, the trend is unlikely to fade away.

Predictive Analytics

Besides automation, another area where AI will have the most impact is future prediction through predictive analytics. AI-powered systems will be able to better predict the outcome and help businesses make better future investments.

At its core, predictive analytics leverages large datasets to identify patterns and relationships that can be used to forecast future outcomes. Businesses use it for things like revenue forecasting, demand planning, and financial performance.

For example, by analyzing previous sales data, a retailer can forecast demand for specific products, helping them optimize stock levels and reduce inventory costs.

Predictive analytics is also finding applications in areas like cybersecurity, application processing, fraud detection and operational efficiency.

Natural Language Processing (NLP)

The reason we're able to converse with a machine is because of NLP. It enables machines to understand, interpret, and generate human language in a way that is both meaningful and useful.

For businesses, NLP is revolutionizing communication, customer service, data analysis, and decision-making by allowing machines to process text and speech just as humans do.

In everyday life, NLP-powered voice assistants like Amazon Alexa, Google Assistant, and Apple's Siri are allowing users to interact with devices through voice commands.

In the future, this trend is likely to expand further and become more useful to both users and businesses.

AI-Driven Decision-Making

As businesses increasingly deal with complex and ever-changing environments, AI-driven decision-making becomes a powerful tool to reduce uncertainty, streamline operations, optimize processes, and drive growth.

One high-risk area where AI-driven decision-making is leaving a mark is trading. JPMorgan Chase uses an AI platform called LOXM to make high-speed trading decisions, executing trades based on real-time market conditions and historical data. This helps the bank optimize trade timing and execution, maximizing profits while minimizing risk.

Another area is supply chain logistics. DHL is using AI systems to predict demand fluctuations, optimize warehouse operations, and even automate route planning for delivery drivers, improving operational efficiency and reducing costs. All of this is without the need for human decision-makers.

The future of AI-driven decision-making is likely to involve a combination of AI systems and human expertise. Rather than replacing humans, AI will serve as a decision-making assistant, providing data-driven insights that empower humans to make better, more informed decisions.

Ethical and Explainable AI

With the rise of AI, skeptics often point out the ethical side of it. And rightly so. Research has found that while AI can streamline recruitment and applicant processing, there is a risk of algorithmic bias, which results in discriminatory hiring practices based on gender, race, color, and personality traits.

Ethical AI refers to the development and deployment of AI systems responsibly and ethically. It involves considering the societal impact of AI, addressing biases, and ensuring fairness and transparency.

Along with Ethical AI, there's a growing trend of explainable AI.

Explainable AI focuses on making AI models more interpretable and understand-able. It involves techniques that allow humans to understand the decision-making process of AI models. In other words, it's about asking the AI model how it arrived at the findings. This enables better inspection of the AI models and ensures there's no inherent bias.

Low-Code/No-Code Machine Learning

Machine learning, a branch of AI, is about teaching computers to learn from data. It's like training a dog – instead of giving it specific commands, you show it examples and let it figure out the pattern.

Traditionally, building ML models requires a deep understanding of programming, data science, and advanced analytics techniques. However, with the rise of low-code and no-code platforms, businesses can build machine learning applications without specialized expertise in coding or data science.

The primary trend driving the adoption of low-code and no-code ML platforms is the democratization of AI and machine learning. As these tools become more accessible, businesses are empowering a wider range of employees—beyond data scientists and engineers—to create ML models. This is breaking down the barrier of entry to AI, enabling business leaders and other non-technical stakeholders to leverage the power of machine learning for decision-making.

Staying Current with AI

AI is evolving rapidly, and new trends and technologies are constantly emerging. For businesses to remain competitive, they must stay informed about the latest developments and integrate them strategically.

However, with the fast-paced nature of AI advancements, it can be a challenge to keep up. Here are some strategies businesses can use to stay updated on AI trends and ensure they don't fall behind.

- Establish a Continuous Learning Culture

One of the most effective ways businesses can stay informed on AI trends is by fostering a culture of continuous learning. This means encouraging employees, especially those in leadership and technical roles, to regularly update their knowledge through training, certifications, and research.

Offer access to online courses, workshops, and certifications focused on AI and related technologies. Platforms like Coursera, edX, Udacity, and LinkedIn Learning provide courses on AI, machine learning, data science, and more.

Also, create an environment where employees can share new insights and developments they've come across in the AI space. This could be through regular team meetings, presentations, or internal knowledge-sharing platforms.

- Subscribe to AI news and journals

Who better to rely on for the latest developments than journalists? There are several industry-leading publications, journals, and websites that publish regular updates on AI innovations, challenges, and opportunities.

Follow websites that track the latest developments in AI, such as TechCrunch, VentureBeat AI, Wired, and The Verge. These sites often feature news, interviews, and expert opinions about new AI trends.

Additionally, many technology companies, research organizations, and consulting firms publish blogs that focus on AI trends within specific industries. For example, McKinsey, Gartner, and Forrester publish research and insights about AI's impact on business and industry-specific applications.

If you're more academia-focused, keep an eye on AI research published in academic journals like the Journal of Artificial Intelligence Research or Nature Machine Intelligence. Reading papers can provide businesses with an in-depth understanding of the latest research and innovations that may impact their operations.

- Attend AI conferences and events

Conferences, webinars, and workshops are excellent opportunities to hear directly from experts, discover cutting-edge technologies, and network with other professionals who are at the forefront of AI innovation.

You can attend or participate in AI-related conferences like the AI Summit, CES (Consumer Electronics Show), Google I/O, and NVIDIA's GPU Technology Conference (GTC). These events often feature announcements about the latest AI trends, product launches, and research breakthroughs.

Conferences provide a platform to meet AI innovators, researchers, and thought leaders. Building relationships with people in the AI field can help businesses get first-hand knowledge of trends and innovations.

Many AI companies and organizations also host workshops or webinars on emerging AI trends and technologies. These sessions can offer practical, hands-on experience and exposure to tools and platforms.

- Collaborate with AI consultants and partners

Hiring consultants with AI expertise can help you assess the latest AI trends and understand how they can apply them to solve their unique challenges. Consultants often guide companies through the process of integrating AI into their operations, recommending the most effective tools and platforms.

Along with experts, you can collaborate with AI technology providers or third-party platforms, such as Google Cloud AI, Microsoft Azure AI, or IBM Watson. These partners often provide updates, white papers, case studies, and even hands-on training for businesses looking to implement AI solutions.

- Monitor AI applications in competitor markets

Keeping an eye on competitors and how they are using AI can help businesses understand which trends are gaining traction and how they can adopt similar technologies to improve their operations.

You can use AI tools to track competitors' AI strategies, such as how they are applying AI in customer support, marketing, sales, or product development. Companies like CB Insights and Crunchbase monitor industry innovations and the AI technologies companies are using. You can leverage the data.

Also, reading real-world case studies about how businesses are successfully implementing AI can provide practical examples and inspiration. Many AI platforms publish detailed case studies showcasing how businesses from different industries are benefiting from AI.

By investing in continuous learning, staying connected to the right sources of information, attending industry events, and working with AI technology partners, you can stay ahead of the curve. And in this ever-evolving world, that's an edge.

Making Your Business AI-Ready

One of the most exciting ways to enhance your business's potential is by embracing AI rather than living in denial. From improving customer service to streamlining operations, AI can help you expand more efficiently and intelligently.

The good news is you don't have to be a tech expert or have a large budget to get started. Becoming AI-ready is all about taking strategic steps to prepare your business, your team, and your processes to harness the power of AI.

A few strategic baby steps will make your business AI-ready.

- Understand the value of AI for your business

The first step toward becoming AI-ready is understanding what AI can do for your specific business. AI isn't a one-size-fits-all solution, and it's essential to focus on the areas where it can have the biggest impact.

Looking to boost sales numbers? Consider starting with AI-powered sales processes. If delivery is backed up, AI can help streamline supply chain management, improve inventory control, and even automate manual tasks to save both time and money.

Thus, adopting AI starts with understanding your own business, and identifying gaps and improvement opportunities.

- Build a solid data foundation

For AI to work effectively, it needs to learn from high-quality, relevant data. Small and mid-sized businesses often overlook the importance of having good data systems in place, but this is crucial when it comes to AI implementation.

For data, Start by gathering customer data, sales data, website interactions, and other business data you already have. Ensure it's clean, structured, and easily accessible. The more consistent your data collection methods, the more effective your AI will be.

Invest in software or systems that can organize and store your data effectively. This could include cloud storage solutions like Google Cloud, which provides data infrastructure.

As your data collection grows, you can invest in data warehouse tools.

- Invest in AI talent

As your business grows and you begin exploring more advanced AI opportunities, having the right talent can make all the difference. Therefore, you should double down on hiring employees that are proficient in using AI tools.

At the bare minimum, look for talent that is acquainted with prompt engineering. Prompt engineering is about conversing with AI to get the desired results. A marketer with prompt engineering skills uses tools like ChatGPT and CoPilot to generate marketing materials faster. Likewise, an accountant with similar skills can crunch numbers faster and be more productive.

Besides that, ensure you provide adequate training through platforms like Udemy and Coursera. This ensures your people are ready to leverage the upcoming AI capabilities for your business.

- Start AI pilot projects

As a new business with limited budgets, you don't need to dive into complex AI projects right away. Start small with solutions that can provide immediate value. There are many accessible and affordable AI tools that can easily integrate into your current operations.

Start with something cost-effective like AI-powered chatbots. Implementing the chatbots on your website can improve customer service and lead generation. Platforms like Tidio, Intercom, or Drift offer easy-to-implement chatbot solutions that don't require a technical background.

Then, you can move to AI-driven marketing and content creation with free tools like ChatGPT.

Begin small and see what works and what doesn't.

Monitor and scale Your AI solutions

Once you have AI tools in place, it's important to regularly monitor their performance and impact on your business. AI systems need ongoing tuning and optimization to remain effective.

Track key performance indicators (KPIs) like customer satisfaction, sales growth, operational efficiency, or employee productivity to gauge the impact of your AI solutions.

Over time, you may need to adjust or retrain your AI models based on new data and trends. Work with your team or AI partners to refine these models and ensure they stay aligned with your business objectives.

Once you start getting measurable positive results, scale operations and improve productivity.

Checklist: Preparing Your Business for AI

There are many checklist you'll find on the internet that help you determine the AI readiness of your business. You're free to use any of them. But for your convenience, I'm providing you my own.

Use this checklist to ensure that your business is fully prepared to integrate and benefit from AI technologies. Whether you're just starting or looking to expand, these steps will guide you toward becoming AI-ready.

1. Understand AI's Potential for Your Business

- Identify key areas where AI can benefit your business (e.g., customer service, sales, operations, data analysis).

- Research AI applications relevant to your industry.

- Define business goals for AI. (e.g., increasing efficiency, improving customer experience, enhancing decision-making).

2. Build a Solid Data Foundation

- Collect and organize business data (customer data, sales data, website analytics, etc.).

- Ensure data quality (clean, accurate, and up-to-date).

- Implement a data management system (cloud storage, CRM, etc.).

- Ensure compliance with data privacy regulations (e.g., GDPR, CCPA).

3. Start with Small, Scalable AI Solutions

- Select easy-to-implement AI tools (e.g., chatbots, email automation, customer analytics).

- Test AI tools on a small scale before full deployment.

- Choose AI solutions with scalability to grow with your business.

4. Invest in AI Talent or Partnerships

- Consider hiring AI professionals (e.g., data scientists, machine learning engineers) if budget allows.

- Work with AI consultants to guide your AI adoption and strategy.

- Explore partnerships with AI firms that specialize in providing solutions for small businesses.

5. Select the Right AI Tools

- Choose AI tools based on your business needs (e.g., CRM software, marketing automation, data analytics tools).

- Evaluate AI platforms that integrate with your existing systems (e.g., POS, eCommerce platforms, marketing tools).

- Ensure the tools are user-friendly, scalable, and secure.

6. Focus on Ethical AI and Transparency

- Ensure your AI tools comply with data protection and privacy laws.

- Select AI tools that are explainable and transparent.

- Be proactive in preventing bias in AI models and algorithms.

7. Establish a Continuous Learning Culture

- Invest in training programs for employees to learn about AI and its applications.

- Encourage employees to stay updated with AI trends and innovations.

- Create a knowledge-sharing platform for team members to exchange insights on AI.

8. Monitor and Optimize AI Performance

- Track KPIs to measure the success of AI implementation (e.g., customer satisfaction, sales growth, operational efficiency).

- Continuously evaluate the effectiveness of AI tools and solutions.

- Optimize and adjust AI models based on new data or business needs.

9. Ensure AI Solutions Are Scalable

- Choose AI platforms and tools that can handle increasing data and complexity as your business grows.

- Plan for AI infrastructure scalability (e.g., cloud computing, modular AI systems).

- Implement AI solutions that can be easily expanded to new departments, products, or markets.

10. Stay Updated on AI Trends

- Subscribe to AI news sources and industry publications (e.g., TechCrunch,

Wired, AI-related blogs).

- Attend AI webinars, conferences, and workshops to stay informed on the latest trends and technologies.

- Network with AI thought leaders and influencers to learn about cutting-edge developments in AI.

Wrap Up

In this final chapter, you explored the incredible potential of AI to future-proof your business. From automating tasks to enhancing customer experiences, integrating AI isn't just about staying competitive—it's about unlocking new efficiencies and creating a business that can adapt to rapid change.

Action Steps

1. Identify one or two areas in your business where AI tools could make an immediate impact.

2. Research and select accessible AI tools to start with, whether for customer service, marketing, or internal processes.

3. Keep learning and adapting as new AI technologies emerge, staying curious about how they can support your business goals.

Up Next

Congratulations! With all these tools and insights, you're now fully equipped to run and grow your business confidently. Remember, each chapter has given you the strategies to face challenges, seize opportunities, and continuously improve. Embrace your entrepreneurial journey with resilience and keep moving forward, knowing you have a solid foundation to build on. Here's to your success!

Conclusion

Now that you're equipped with all the knowledge to start and scale your business, it's important to recall a crucial adage, "Business is a marathon, not a sprint." What this conveys is that you should always think long-term and run your business with a vision.

That vision should always have a strong foundation, which was the focus of Chapter 2. A strong foundation will absorb the tremors of all the mistakes you'll likely make along the way. This is something failed entrepreneurs learn the hard way. Make sure you don't walk their paths. Before anything else, invest adequate time in building a strong foundation.

While the foundation serves as the base, it's bland without confidence and charisma. The leaders, whether in business, politics, or sports, you follow are likely pretty charismatic and carry an aura with them wherever they go. While not mandatory, this is essential.

Successful leaders are also very accountable. They have high accounting standards and hold everyone on their team accountable, including themselves.

Talking of everyone, you revisit another business adage, "Take care of your people, they will take care of the business." The people in your team are more than just a group of individuals. A team is a dynamic entity capable of achieving extraordinary results when nurtured and empowered.

So invest time in building trust, fostering open communication, and recognizing and rewarding achievements. Lead by example, empower your team members, and create a positive and supportive work environment. Remember, a high-performing team is a valuable asset that can propel your business to new heights.

We've also touched deeply on AI concepts. It's important to remember that technology, while powerful, is merely a tool. The true magic lies in how you wield it. It's a combination of technological prowess, strategic thinking, and human ingenuity. By understanding the core principles of AI and its potential applications, you can unlock a universe of possibilities for your business.

AI will become even more core to your business as you scale, which you invariably will. After all, what separates successful businesses from failed ones is they are able to scale and seize new market opportunities.

As we talked about in Chapter 7, seizing new opportunities starts with deep and continuous market research. Just to reiterate (because I see business owners making this mistake time and time again), market research isn't merely a box to tick; it's the compass that guides your business toward uncharted territories. By consistently monitoring industry trends, analyzing consumer behavior, and staying abreast of emerging technologies, you can gain a competitive edge.

As we wrap up this ebook, the last piece of advice I'd give you is to enjoy the process. Because if you don't, you'll feel like giving up every single day. And one morning, you'll quit and start applying for jobs, a path you left behind to fulfill your dreams.

So march ahead with enthusiasm, plan diligently, be grounded, and serve your customers the best you can.

If you got value out of this ebook and liked what I had to say, consider leaving a review. It helps me as an author and others like you find the content that perhaps they desperately need!

LEAVE A REVIEW!

SCAN ME

References

3 Inspiring Startup Success Stories | HBS Online. (2023, August 31). Business Insights Blog. https://online.hbs.edu/blog/post/startup-stories

4 financial indicators every entrepreneur should monitor. (2024, October 29). *B DC.ca.* https://www.bdc.ca/en/articles-tools/money-finance/manage-finances/5-key-indicators-monitor

6 Best AI-Powered Business Plan Generators (December 2023) | Bizway Resources. (n.d.). https://www.bizway.io/blog/best-ai-business-plan-generators

7 Proven strategies to overcome fear of starting a business. (n.d.). https://www.candicemontgomeryonline.com/blog/fear-of-starting-business

8 Incredibly inspiring examples of online brand communities | Disciple. (n.d.). https://www.disciplemedia.com/engaging-your-community/8-brand-communities-examples/

11 great brand community examples for 2024 | Khoros. (n.d.). https://khoros.com/blog/brand-community-examples

13 Finance Experts Recommend Tech Tools For Managing Business And Personal Finances. (2023, February 27). Forbes. https://www.forbes.com/sites/forbesfinancecouncil/2023/02/27/13-finance-experts-recommend-tech-tools-for-managing-business-and-personal-finances/?sh=435f6e1a746f

28 Free SEO tools to boost your search rankings in 2024. (n.d.). Buffer: All-you-need Social Media Toolkit for Small Businesses. https://buffer.com/library/free-seo-tools/

Aastha. (2023, May 24). *Rising from the Ground Up 10 Inspiring Startup Success Stories*. Silicon Valley Innovation Center. https://siliconvalley.center/blog/rising-from-the-ground-up-10-inspiring-startup-success-stories

Admin. (2024, August 22). The role of artificial intelligence (AI) in cybersecurity: Enhancing threat detection and response - Atlantic Data Security. *Atlantic Data Security*. https://atlanticdatasecurity.com/blog/ai-cybersecurity-threat-detection/

Adobe Communications Team. (2022, September 2). *Email Marketing — a step-by-step guide to getting started*. Adobe Experience Cloud. https://business.adobe.com/blog/basics/guide-to-email-marketing

Advania UK. (2024, July 23). *How to choose the right technology for your business - Advania*. https://www.advania.co.uk/insights/blog/how-to-choose-the-right-technology-for-your-business/

Advertising & Signage. (n.d.). Stanton. https://www.stantonca.gov/departments/public_safety/code_enforcement/advertising___signage.php

Aghina, W., Handscomb, C., Salo, O., & Thaker, S. (2021, May 25). *The impact of agility: How to shape your organization to compete*. McKinsey & Company. https://www.mckinsey.com/capabilities/people-and-organizational-performance/our-insights/the-impact-of-agility-how-to-shape-your-organization-to-compete

Ahmed, A. (2024a, February 15). *Audience engagement: What it is and tips to improve it*. Sprout Social. https://sproutsocial.com/insights/audience-engagement/

Ahmed, A. (2024b, June 17). *20 of the best social media analytics tools for your brand in 2024*. Sprout Social. https://sproutsocial.com/insights/social-media-analytics-tools/

Ai, G. (2023, October 31). *The Role of AI in streamlining Business Processes and Increasing Efficiency*. https://www.linkedin.com/pulse/role-ai-streamlining-business-processes-increasing-efficiency-nxakf/

AI readiness checklist | Collibra. (n.d.). Collibra. https://www.collibra.com/us/en/resources/ai-readiness-checklist

AI ready. (n.d.-a). https://www.launchconsulting.com/airedy-assessment

AI ready. (n.d.-b). https://www.launchconsulting.com/airedy-assessment

AI Tax Software - Top AI tools. (n.d.). TopAI.tools. https://topai.tools/s/AI-tax-so ftware

AI Your Marketing Analytics: 5 Innovative Ways to Leverage AI for Deeper data Insights. (n.d.). https://improvado.io/blog/ai-marketing-analytics

AI-Driven Market Analysis: Revolutionizing financial insights for AMEX:SPY by JS_TechTrading — TradingView. (2023, November 27). TradingView. https://www.tradingview.com/chart/SPY/V9OQ3yrL-AI-Driven-Market-Analysis-Revolutionizing-Financial-Insights/

Alagar. (2023, November 2). The intersection of AI and business analytics. *IABAC®.* https://iabac.org/blog/the-intersection-of-ai-and-business-analytics

Alblooshi, N. (2023, April 17). *How AI is Transforming the Financial Sector: Case Studies from UAE and around the World.* https://www.linkedin.com/pulse/how-ai-transforming-financial-sector-case-studies-from-alblooshi/

Alibaba.com. (2021, June 29). *Home-based business: 6 advantages and disadvantages.* Alibaba.com Seller Central. https://seller.alibaba.com/businessblogs/pxdod 30u-home-based-business-6-advantages-and-disadvantages

AllBusiness Editors. (n.d.). *Top 10 Advantages of a Home-Based Business.* allBusiness: Your Small Business Advantage. https://www.allbusiness.com/top-10-advantages -of-a-home-based-business-11087-1.html

Amaresan, S. (2024, June 4). How to Make Money on Social Media [New Data + Case Studies]. *HubSpot.* https://blog.hubspot.com/marketing/social-media-shopp ing-case-studies

Ambrozi, A. (2023, October 24). *11 Challenges of Adopting AI in Business (And How to Address Them Head-On).* Forbes. https://www.forbes.com/sites/forbesbusinesscouncil/2023/10/24/11-challenges-o f-adopting-ai-in-business-and-how-to-address-them-head-on/?sh=1d15d1934bfe

Anand, S. (2022, November 11). *7 common entrepreneur-ial fears and how to overcome them – Early Growth*. Early Growth. https://earlygrowthfinancialservices.com/blog/7-common-entrepreneur ial-fears-and-how-to-overcome-them-early-growth/

Anthony, S. D. (2022, November 1). *The top 20 business transformations of the last decade*. Harvard Business Review. https://hbr.org/2019/09/the-top-20-business-t ransformations-of-the-last-decade

Api, & Api. (2024, May 7). *Tax Compliance Checklist | Process Street*. Process Street. https://www.process.st/templates/tax-compliance-checklist/

Artificial intelligence in fintech: Use cases and examples. (n.d.). https://www.itransi tion.com/ai/fintech

Arun, R. (2024, November 6). *What is Digital Marketing and How Does It Work?* Simplilearn.com. https://www.simplilearn.com/tutorials/digital-marketing-tutori al/what-is-digital-marketing

Athuraliya, A. (2023, January 5). *5 Gap analysis tools to identify and close the gaps in your business*. Creately Blog. https://creately.com/blog/strategy-and-planning/gap -analysis-tools/

Author_Name. (1970, January 1). *post_title*. U Of I Tax School. https://taxschool.illinois.edu/post/leveraging-the-power-of-chatgpt-and -other-ai-tools-in-your-tax-practice/

Autoness Media. (2024, January 23). *Top 10 AI tools for Business: 2024's G a m e - C h a n g e r s .* https://www.linkedin.com/pulse/top-10-ai-tools-business-2024s-game-changers-a utonessmedia-qfijf/?trk=article-ssr-frontend-pulse_more-articles_related-content-c ard

B, S. (2023, February 27). *5 Reasons Having an Online Presence is Essential in Today's Modern Business World*. https://www.linkedin.com/pulse/5-reasons-having-onlin e-presence-essential-todays-modern-barnwell/

Bajpai, P. (2023, December 20). *Pros and cons of a Limited Liability Company (LLC)*. Investopedia. https://www.investopedia.com/articles/investing/091014/basics-forming-limited-liability-company-llc.asp

Bakersfield.com. (2021, May 17). Key Components of Traditional Business Plans. https://www.bakersfield.com/kern-business-journal/key-components-of-traditional-business-plans/article_29b786f2-b1a7-11eb-be75-670fd587aadd.html

Banners / Wind Devices | Garland, TX. (n.d.). https://www.garlandtx.gov/2162/Banners-Wind-Devices#:~:text=Banner%20Permits&text=Permitted%20temporary%20banners%20may%20have,area%20exceed%2080%20square%20feet.

Bautista, M. (2023, March 1). *The Impact of Machine Learning on Business Processes - Digital CXO*. Digital CxO. https://digitalcxo.com/article/the-impact-of-machine-learning-on-business-processes/

Beautiful business & accounting software. (n.d.). Xero. https://www.xero.com/us/

Berger, B. (2024, September 26). *The 6 elements of the content marketing process*. Search Engine Journal. https://www.searchenginejournal.com/content-marketing-process-elements/376908/

Best AI Financial Forecasting Tools - AI Tools Network. (2023, July 3). AI Tools Network. https://aitoolsnetwork.com/tools/financial-forecasting/

Blunt, W. (2018, March 8). 9 Key elements of an effective social media marketing strategy, and how to establish them. *Social Media Today*. https://www.socialmediatoday.com/news/9-key-elements-of-an-effective-social-media-marketing-strategy-and-how-to/518639/

Brown, L. (2024, November 12). *Become a successful SMM in 10 steps*. Filmora. https://filmora.wondershare.com/more-tips/become-a-successful-smm.html

Build a scalable business model: Strategies and best practices | Mailchimp. (n.d.). Mailchimp. https://mailchimp.com/resources/scalable-business/

Business plan template for a startup business. (n.d.). SCORE. https://www.score.o rg/resource/template/business-plan-template-a-startup-business

Business Tax Basics for Beginners. (n.d.). The Hartford. https://www.thehartford.c om/business-insurance/strategy/business-taxes

Case Studies. (n.d.). Zinia. https://zinia.ai/casestudies/

Case Study – Enabling Operational Efficiency through process and Technology Transformation during Growth - SIKICH. (2024, April 3). Sikich. https://www.sikich.com/insight/case-study-enabling-operational-efficiency -through-process-and-technology-transformation-during-growth/

Catherine. (2024, April 29). 10 Best AI tax Software for Business in 2024 (Ditch the spreadsheet). *AI Mojo.* https://aimojo.pro/ai-tax-softwares/

Chacko, A. (2024, May 15). *5 overlooked B2B market research methods for understanding your customers.* Sprout Social. https://sproutsocial.com/insights/b2b-ma rket-research/

Chaffey, D. (2024, July 11). *Digital marketing strategy template - free planning tool. 2024 edition.* Smart Insights. https://www.smartinsights.com/digital-marketing-st rategy/digital-marketing-strategy-and-planning-template/

Charrington, D. (2024, November 21). Top 18 market research tools (Free & Paid): A buyer's guide. *Qualaroo Blog - User Research and Customer Feedback Trends.* https://qualaroo.com/blog/market-research-tools/

Chodipilli, K. (2023, July 13). *5 Reasons Why Agility is More Important Than Ever in the Enterprise.* Leadership Tribe US. https://leadershiptribe.com/blog/5-reason s-why-agility-is-more-important-than-ever-in-the-enterprise

Choosing the Right Technology Strategy For Your Business A Comprehensive Guide. (2024, June 14). Faster Capital. https://fastercapital.com/content/Choosing-the -Right-Technology-Strategy-For-Your-Business--A-Comprehensive-Guide.html

CMO's Guide to Email Marketing ROI. (2024, September 3). Litmus. https://ww w.litmus.com/resources/email-marketing-roi

Content Marketing — definition, types, and how to do it. (2023, May 23). *Adobe Experience Cloud Team.* https://business.adobe.com/blog/basics/content-marketing

Contributor, S. (2021, March 5). 5 ways to engage consumers on social media. *Forbes.* https://www.forbes.com/sites/square/2020/12/04/5-ways-to-engage-consumers-on-social-media/?sh=1ccd6273b3f4

Conway, S. (2023, June 21). *The role of AI in streamlining business operations.* https://www.linkedin.com/pulse/role-ai-streamlining-business-operations-sean-conway/

CoSchedule. (2024, October 30). *SMART Marketing Goal Examples for 2024.* CoSchedule Blog. https://coschedule.com/marketing-strategy/marketing-goals/smart-marketing-goal-examples

Craig, L. (2024, August 26). *10 top AI and machine learning trends for 2024.* Search Enterprise AI. https://www.techtarget.com/searchenterpriseai/tip/9-top-AI-and-machine-learning-trends

Creative and innovative ways to fund a business startup. (2024, June 26). Faster Capital. https://fastercapital.com/content/Creative-and-innovative-ways-to-fund-a-business-startup.html

Daley, S. (2024a, February 27). *13 blockchain companies paving the way for the future.* Built In. https://builtin.com/blockchain/blockchain-companies-roundup

Daley, S. (2024b, November 6). *76 Artificial intelligence examples shaking up business across industries.* Built In. https://builtin.com/artificial-intelligence/examples-ai-in-industry

Dallos, M. (2024, May 3). Business Modell Evolution - by BMC | M. Dallos. *Business Model Company.* https://businessmodel.company/business-model-evolution/

Das, S. (2022, December 12). *Business agility - why it's important and how to achieve it.* https://www.linkedin.com/pulse/business-agility-why-its-important-how-achieve-soumitri-das/

Davis, B. (2023, September 11). *Forbes.* AI in Accounting and Bookkeeping: Braving the New Digital Frontier. https://www.forbes.com/sites/forbestechcouncil/2023/09/11/ai-in-accounting-and-bookkeeping-braving-the-new-digital-frontier/?sh=4f318458350b

Davis, M. (2024a, September 27). *Identifying and managing business risks.* Investopedia. https://www.investopedia.com/articles/financial-theory/09/risk-management-business.asp

Davis, M. (2024b, October 17). *How to overcome the fear of financial risk when starting your own business.* Qonto - Blog. https://qonto.com/en/blog/creators/tools-tips/how-to-overcome-the-fear-of-financial-risk-when-starting-your-own-business

DeBellis, D. (2023, October 31). *Why Adaptability is the New Digital Transformation.* WGI. https://wginc.com/why-adaptability-is-the-new-digital-transformation/

Decker, A. (2024, August 21). Accounting 101: Accounting Basics for Beginners to Learn. *HubSpot.* https://blog.hubspot.com/sales/accounting-101

DeMarco, J., & Anthony, L. (2024, November 18). *Startup funding: What it is and how to get capital for a business.* NerdWallet. https://www.nerdwallet.com/article/small-business/startup-funding

Developer, W. (2024, November 22). *14 Financial Management Tools that Every Business Must Have.* Cflow. https://www.cflowapps.com/top-financial-management-tools/

Dialpad. (2024, June 6). *11 AI tools for small businesses (Low cost, big impact!).* https://www.dialpad.com/blog/ai-tools-for-small-business/

Discover the Domo Data Experience Platform | DoMo. (n.d.). https://www.domo.com/

Doepping, A. (2024, July 31). *Your 2023 Financial Health Checklist: Set yourself up for success.* Lafayette Federal Credit Union. https://www.lfcu.org/news/managing-money-credit/your-2023-financial-health-checklist-set-yourself-up-for-success-this-year-with-our-financial-health-checklist/

Dua, M. (2024, October 29). *17 AI tools for small businesses to become more Productive*. Mailmodo. https://www.mailmodo.com/guides/ai-tools-for-small-businesses/

Due.com. (n.d.). 5 Ways Companies can pursue financial Sustainability. *Nasdaq*. https://www.nasdaq.com/articles/5-ways-companies-can-pursue-financial-sustainability

Edmond, R. (2024, July 11). Defining and achieving authentic engagement. *GaggleAMP*. https://blog.gaggleamp.com/what-is-authentic-engagement

Experts, D. (2023, August 10). *Revenue diversification*. DealHub. https://dealhub.io/glossary/revenue-diversification/

Farese, D. (2024, February 21). Market Research: A How-To Guide and Template. *HubSpot*. https://blog.hubspot.com/marketing/market-research-buyers-journey-guide#template

Feedspot. (2024, November 12). *Top 60 Tech Forums in 2024*. FeedSpot for Forum Lists and Online Message Boards. https://forums.feedspot.com/technology_forums/

Finance AI Tools. (n.d.). TopAI.tools. https://topai.tools/filter?t=finance

Flower, D. (2023, July 25). *The Power of Machine Learning: The Business Impact on Real-Time Data*. Forbes. https://www.forbes.com/sites/forbestechcouncil/2023/07/25/the-power-of-machine-learning-the-business-impact-on-real-time-data/?sh=7987302963b6

Forbes. (2023, September 11). The Future of Artificial Intelligence: Predictions and Trends. https://www.forbes.com/sites/forbesagencycouncil/2023/09/11/the-future-of-artificial-intelligence-predictions-and-trends/?sh=49ea95d12393

Fox, J. (2017, October 17). *Six factors to consider when choosing a business location | Virgin*. Virgin.com. https://www.virgin.com/about-virgin/latest/six-factors-consider-when-choosing-location-your-business

Fredrick, M. (2023, April 18). *10 Proven tactics to engage and attract your target audience online*. https://www.linkedin.com/pulse/10-proven-tactics-engage-attrac t-your-target-audience-marube-fredrick

FreshBooks. (2024, July 23). *12 Legal requirements for starting a small business*. htt ps://www.freshbooks.com/hub/startup/starting-small-business-legal-requirements

Friedman, O. (2023, March 28). *Using technology in business for insights and strategy*. Forbes. https://www.forbes.com/sites/forbesbusinesscouncil/2023/03/28/us ing-technology-in-business-for-insights-and-strategy/?sh=52c819126284

Gadjev, B. (2023, May 9). *7 Strategies for improving operational efficiency in any small and medium-sized business*. https://www.linkedin.com/pulse/7-strategies-improvi ng-operational-efficiency-any-small-bobby-gadjev/

GeeksforGeeks. (2024, July 23). *10 Best Budgeting Tools 2024 [Free]*. GeeksforGeeks. https://www.geeksforgeeks.org/ai-tools-for-personal-finance-managem ent-and-budgeting/

GoldenLink: Marketing Coaching & Training. (2023, April 26). *5 Essential Tips for Building Authentic Engagement with Your Audience*. https://www.linkedin.com/p ulse/5-essential-tips-building-authentic-engagement-your-audience/

Gomez, R. (2024, June 6). *The importance of social media marketing: 7 stats that prove social's role in business success*. Sprout Social. https://sproutsocial.com/insigh ts/importance-of-social-media-marketing-in-business/

Gonzalez, J. (n.d.). *Why is having an online presence important for a small business*. allBusiness: Your Small Business Advantage. https://www.allbusiness.com/why-is -online-presence-important-for-a-business

Graber, N. (n.d.). *Why are SMART Goals Necessary In Business? | MileIQ*. https: //mileiq.com/blog-en-gb/smart-business-goals

Gravel, A., & Gravel, A. (2024, September 19). *17 examples of strong brand storytelling (updated 2024) - Toast Studio*. Toast Studio. https://www.toaststudio.com/ en/articles/pg-volvo-and-other-examples-of-strong-brand-storytelling/

Great Learning. (2024, September 3). The fundamentals of digital marketing. *Great Learning Blog: Free Resources What Matters to Shape Your Career!* https://www.m ygreatlearning.com/blog/the-fundamentals-of-digital-marketing/

Griswold, D. (2024, March 22). *What is an LLC? Definition and steps on how to form an LLC.* https://www.wolterskluwer.com/en/expert-insights/how-to-form-a n-llc-what-is-an-llc-advantages-disadvantages-and-more

Haan, K. (2024, October 31). *How to start a business in 11 steps (2024 guide).* Forbes Advisor. https://www.forbes.com/advisor/business/how-to-start-a-business/

Haije, E. G. (2024, September 12). *Top 29 Best Customer Feedback Tools in 2024.* Mopinion. https://mopinion.com/customer-feedback-tools/

Han, S. (2024, August 23). *6 Market research benefits for your business.* Sago. https ://sago.com/en/resources/blog/what-are-the-business-benefits-of-market-research/

Harnish, B. (2021, April 30). *The 11 most important parts of SEO you need to get right.* Search Engine Journal. https://www.searchenginejournal.com/most-import ant-parts-of-seo/254225/

Harper, J. (2023, October 23). Machine Learning for Real-Time Data Analysis: Training models in production. *The New Stack.* https://thenewstack.io/machine -learning-for-real-time-data-analysis-training-models-in-production/

Harris, M. (2023, March 29). *Why adaptability is an essential business strategy.* https://www.linkedin.com/pulse/why-adaptability-essential-business-strategy -mikki-harris/

Hassan, A. U., CPA. (2023, May 7). *The importance of budgeting for business success.* https://www.linkedin.com/pulse/importance-budgeting-business-success-am mar-ul-hassan/

Heaslip, E. (2023, September 5). *How to use AI tools to write a business plan.* CO- by US Chamber of Commerce. https://www.uschamber.com/co/start/startup/ai-too ls-to-write-a-business-plan

Hegde, S. (2024, January 24). *Top 10 AI Marketing Tools that Can Increase Return-On-Ad-Spend.* https://www.linkedin.com/pulse/top-10-ai-marketing-tools-can-increase-shreeharsha-hegde/

Herzing University. (2020, May 18). A guide to setting up a dedicated workspace at home. *Herzing University.* https://www.herzing.edu/blog/guide-setting-dedicated-workspace-home

Hesseln, H. (2020, May 14). *4 Real-Life examples of successful change management in business.* https://www.linkedin.com/pulse/4-real-life-examples-successful-change-management-business-hesseln/

Higgins, M. (2021, May 19). *The Future Of Accounting: How Will Digital Transformation Impact Accountants?* Forbes. https://www.forbes.com/sites/forbestechcouncil/2021/05/19/the-future-of-accounting-how-will-digital-transformation-impact-accountants/?sh=5ec188e153fb

Hilson, S. (2023, September 15). *AI market Research: Tools, techniques, and trends.* Rock Content. https://rockcontent.com/blog/ai-market-research/

Home-Based business statistics to know going in 2023. (n.d.). Bizee. https://bizee.com/blog/post/shocking-us-home-based-business-statistics

Home-Based entrepreneur Stories. (2024). Home Business. https://homebusinessmag.com/categories/success-stories-lifestyles/

Hop. (2024, January 9). *Top 7 AI startups Revolutionizing data science and analytics.* https://www.linkedin.com/pulse/top-7-ai-startups-revolutionizing-data-science-analytics-hophr-xbnpe/

How AI can scale personalization and creativity in Marketing - SPONSOR CONTENT FROM INTUIT MAILCHIMP. (2023, August 17). Harvard Business Review. https://hbr.org/sponsored/2023/08/how-ai-can-scale-personalization-and-creativity-in-marketing

How can you create content that reflects your company's values and mission? (2023, September 27). https://www.linkedin.com/advice/0/how-can-you-create-content-reflects-your-companys

How can you ensure sustainable cost management strategies? (2023, September 18). https://www.linkedin.com/advice/0/how-can-you-ensure-sustainable-cost-m anagement-strategies

How can you use storytelling to maintain brand identity consistency? (2023, September 13). https://www.linkedin.com/advice/0/how-can-you-use-storytelling-maint ain-brand-identity

How To Create A Company Culture Of Continuous Learning And Development. (2023, April 24). Forbes. https://www.forbes.com/sites/forbeshumanresourcescouncil/2023/04/24/how-to -create-a-company-culture-of-continuous-learning-and-development/?sh=756c280 1387d

How to create a social media marketing strategy | Mailchimp. (n.d.). Mailchimp. https://mailchimp.com/resources/how-to-market-on-social-media/?ds_c=DEPT_ AOC_Google_Search_ROW_EN_NB_UpRet_Broad_50off_T5&ds_kids=p783 77605262&ds_a_lid=aud-1549074331369:dsa-1543646106214&ds_cid=7170000 0115522798&ds_agid=58700008586041932&gad_source=1&gclid=CjwKCAiA 3JCvBhA8EiwA4kujZlOqvYpS-Q5kobnF35IQHA25LthSTrinbx8JO8Sa9gAh9et Ss1YSwRoCU3sQAvD_BwE&gclsrc=aw.ds

How to register a business in the US | Stripe. (2023, April 6). https://stripe.com/res ources/more/how-to-register-a-business-in-the-us

How to Scale a business: 6 Tactics to Utilize | HBS Online. (2019, March 7). Business Insights Blog. https://online.hbs.edu/blog/post/how-to-scale-a-business

How to scale a business and proven techniques to do so. (n.d.). Tony Robbins. https:/ /www.tonyrobbins.com/career-business/mindful-scaling/

How to stay Up-to-Date on tech trends and innovations | IronHack Blog. (n.d.) . https://www.ironhack.com/us/blog/how-to-stay-up-to-date-on-tech-trends-and -innovations

How To Write a Business Plan: Seven Elements | Infographic. (2023, January 18). University of Arizona Global Campus. https://www.uagc.edu/blog/how-write-business-plan-step-by-step

Howarth, J. (2024, November 21). 9 Best trend analysis software Tools (Detailed Overview). *Exploding Topics.* https://explodingtopics.com/blog/trend-analysis-software

Huston, H. (2023, November 3). *Single-member LLC vs. sole proprietorship: Advantages & disadvantages.* https://www.wolterskluwer.com/en/expert-insights/single-member-llc-vs-sole-proprietorship

Improving Operational Efficiencies: 4 Success stories in Digital transformation. (n.d.). https://www.techtarget.com/searchcio/MulticloudbyDesign/Improving-Operational-Efficiencies-4-Success-Stories-in-Digital-Transformation

Indeed Editorial Team. (2023, July 31). *7 Reasons Why Budgeting Is Vital for Successful Businesses.* Indeed. https://www.indeed.com/career-advice/career-development/why-budget-is-important

Indeed Editorial Team. (2024a, February 12). *How To Stay Current With Technology Trends.* Indeed. https://www.indeed.com/career-advice/career-development/keeping-up-with-technology

Indeed Editorial Team. (2024b, August 15). *10 Methods of Market Research.* Indeed. https://www.indeed.com/career-advice/career-development/methods-of-market-research

Indeed Editorial Team. (2024c, August 18). *10 Pros and Cons of Being in a Business Partnership.* Indeed. https://www.indeed.com/career-advice/career-development/pros-cons-of-business-partnership

InfoDesk. (n.d.). Market Insights Strategy: Traditional Research vs. AI-Driven Analysis. © *2024 InfoDesk. All Rights. Reserved.* https://www.infodesk.com/blog/market-insights-strategy-traditional-research-vs.-ai-driven-analysis

Infragist. (2023, October 26). *How AI and ML enhance cybersecurity in the business world*. https://www.linkedin.com/pulse/how-ai-ml-enhance-cybersecurity-busine ss-world-infragist-n5mre/

Ingov, P. (2024, October 13). *Data Storytelling Enhanced with AI: Tools and Courses*. ingoStudio. https://ingostudio.com/storytelling/data-storytelling/

Jagtap, A. (2024, September 13). *The Top 13 AI Business Plan Generators: A 2024 Guide*. Upmetrics. https://upmetrics.co/blog/ai-business-plan-generators

Jansons, K. (2024, September 8). *AI in Finance and Banking: Use Cases in 2024*. MindTitan. https://mindtitan.com/resources/industry-use-cases/ai-use-cases-in-fi nance-and-banking/

Jarboe, G. (2024, January 16). AI-enhanced YouTube marketing: Insights from 3 case studies. *Search Engine Land*. https://searchengineland.com/ai-youtube-mark eting-insights-case-studies-436536

Jegou, S. (2024, August 29). *How is IoT disrupting major industries– Benefits, Applications and Use-Cases*. Transatel. https://www.transatel.com/news-and-insights /blog/iot-disrupted-industries-applications/

Jhajharia, S. (2024, August 2). The importance of creating a scalable business model - Growth Idea Ltd. *Growth Idea Ltd*. https://growthidea.co.uk/blog/the-importa nce-of-creating-a-scalable-business-model

Jobanputra, K. (2023, April 18). You have to take risks to succeed. Here are 4 Risk-Taking benefits in entrepreneurship. *Entrepreneur*. https://www.entrepreneur.com/starting-a-business/want-success-you-have-t o-take-risks-4-benefits-of/449208

Johnson, J. (2024, October 30). *Would you make it on Shark Tank? The importance of scalable business models*. business.com. https://www.business.com/articles/the-i mportance-of-scalable-business-models/

Jones, S. (2024, February 2). *AI's Impact on Brand Storytelling: Crafting Compelling Narratives in 2024*. https://www.linkedin.com/pulse/ais-impact-brand-storytelling-crafting-compellin

g-narratives-jones-4pvwe/?trk=article-ssr-frontend-pulse_more-articles_related-content-card

Jordan, J. (2023, March 1). *The Power of Scaling: Why it's important for your business*. https://www.linkedin.com/pulse/power-scaling-why-its-important-your-business-jim-jordan/

Joy, K. (2023, May 17). *Optimizing Operational Efficiency with Generative AI: A Case Study*. https://www.linkedin.com/pulse/optimizing-operational-efficiency-generative-ai-case-study-kevin-joy-/

Kantrow, A. (2014, August 1). *The Strategy-Technology connection*. Harvard Business Review. https://hbr.org/1980/07/the-strategy-technology-connection

Kart, R. (2023, July 12). *Crafting a Narrative: the crucial role of storytelling in an AI-Driven future*. https://www.linkedin.com/pulse/crafting-narrative-crucial-role-storytelling-ai-driven-randy-kart/

Kaur, F. P. (2024, October 23). *10 Creative AI in Marketing Examples and Use Cases*. Mailmodo. https://www.mailmodo.com/guides/ai-in-marketing-examples/

Kelly, R. (2023, June 1). *Market research: an important investment for Long-Term viability*. Forbes. https://www.forbes.com/sites/forbestechcouncil/2023/06/01/market-research-an-important-investment-for-long-term-viability/?sh=d910204551bc

Kenan, J., & Kenan, J. (2024, November 18). *Social media analytics: The complete guide*. Sprout Social. https://sproutsocial.com/insights/social-media-analytics/

Kenton, W. (2024, June 22). *Organizational structure for companies with examples and benefits*. Investopedia. https://www.investopedia.com/terms/o/organizational-structure.asp

Kirk, R. S. (2022, January 6). *Commentary: American businesses need to invest in tech education*. Fortune. https://fortune.com/2022/01/06/american-businesses-need-to-invest-in-tech-education-skills-gap-labor-shortage-verizon-csr-rose-stuckey-kirk/

Kirschenbaum, E. (2024, October 4). *How to Register a business in the USA in 7 easy steps [2023]*. https://pay.com/blog/how-to-register-a-business-in-usa

Krissansen, J. (2023, July 12). *12 ways to find the perfect angel investor - Finmark*. Finmark. https://finmark.com/how-to-find-angel-investors/

Kumar, K. (2023, May 7). *Embracing change: The importance of adaptability in a Fast-Paced technological world*. https://www.linkedin.com/pulse/embracing-change-importance-adaptability-fast-paced-world-kumar/

Lake, R. (2024, June 3). *Your annual financial planning checklist*. Investopedia. https://www.investopedia.com/articles/personal-finance/your-annual-financial-planning-check-list.asp

LegalNature. (2024). Tax Obligations for Each Business Type. https://www.legalnature.com/guides/an-overview-of-tax-obligations-for-each-business-type

Lin, P. (2022, September 2). AI-Based Marketing Personalization: How Machines Analyze Your Audience. *Artificial Intelligence*. https://www.marketingaiinstitute.com/blog/ai-based-marketing-personalization

Livolsi, K. (2023, October 16). *Diversifying revenue streams - Strategies for business stability and growth*. https://www.linkedin.com/pulse/diversifying-revenue-streams-strategies-business-growth-livolsi/

Llc, B. A. (2023, April 25). *Fostering a more engaged and knowledgeable tech community*. https://www.linkedin.com/pulse/fostering-more-engaged-knowledgeable-tech-community/

Llp, I. I. (2023, August 24). *Digital Marketing Fundamentals: A Beginner's Guide for new businesses*. https://www.linkedin.com/pulse/digital-marketing-fundamentals-beginners-guide-new-businesses/

Loktionova, M. (2023a, January 26). *Brand Storytelling: The Definitive 2024 Guide (with Examples)*. Semrush Blog. https://www.semrush.com/blog/definitive-guide-to-brand-storytelling/

Loktionova, M. (2023b, June 12). *Content marketing for small businesses: 9 essential tips*. Semrush Blog. https://www.semrush.com/blog/content-marketing-for-small -businesses/

Ltd, T. a. P. (2023, April 21). *10 ways to Foster a Culture of Continuous Learning in Your Company*. https://www.linkedin.com/pulse/10-ways-foster-culture-conti nuous-learning-your/

Lyons, A. (2023, July 6). *A Step-By-Step Process For Implementing AI In A Small Business.*   Forbes. https://www.forbes.com/sites/forbesbusinessdevelopmentcouncil/2023/07/06/a-s tep-by-step-process-for-implementing-ai-in-a-small-business/?sh=240ed08d55d0

Machine Learning Market Size, Share, Growth | Trends [2030]. (n.d.). https://ww w.fortunebusinessinsights.com/machine-learning-market-102226

Machine Learning Startups funded by Y Combinator (YC) 2024 | Y Combinator. (n.d.). Y Combinator. https://www.ycombinator.com/companies/industry/mach ine-learning

March, L. (2024, September 3). *9 Highly successful market research examples*. Sim-ilarweb. https://www.similarweb.com/blog/research/market-research/market-rese arch-examples/

Market Trends, & Market Trends. (2022, March 1). *AI-Powered Market Research: What are the benefits?* Analytics Insight. https://www.analyticsinsight.net/ai-pow ered-market-research-what-are-the-benefits/

Markets, R. A. (2022, September 28). Global digital advertising and marketing market to reach $786.2 billion by 2026 at a CAGR of 13.9%. *GlobeNewswire News R   o   o   m   .* https://www.globenewswire.com/news-release/2022/09/28/2524217/28124/en/ Global-Digital-Advertising-and-Marketing-Market-to-Reach-786-2-Billion-by-202 6-at-a-CAGR-of-13-9.html#:~:text=Amid%20the%20COVID%2D19%20crisis%2 C%20the%20global%20market,Players:%20Acxiom%20Corporation.%20Alibaba% 20Group%20Holding%20Limited.

Marr, B. (2021, July 13). *The 10 best examples of how companies use artificial intelligence in practice*. Bernard Marr. https://bernardmarr.com/the-10-best-examples-o f-how-companies-use-artificial-intelligence-in-practice/

Martinuzzi, B. (2023, June 23). *The advantages and disadvantages of a business partnership*. Business Class: Trends and Insights | American Express. https://www.americanexpress.com/en-us/business/trends-and-insights/arti cles/what-are-the-advantages-and-disadvantages-of-a-partnership/

Maslan, A. (2024, January 24). *What are the Most Common Business Expansion Strategy Mistakes?* Pinnacle Global Network. https://pinnacleglobalnetwork.com /what-are-the-most-common-business-expansion-strategy-mistakes/

McCue, I. (2020, October 21). *15 Key Financial Metrics & KPIs for Small Businesses*. Oracle NetSuite. https://www.netsuite.com/portal/resource/articles/financ ial-management/small-business-financial-metrics.shtml

Michaelis, C. (2023, July 12). *Fearless entrepreneurship: tackling your fears and unlocking your potential*. https://www.linkedin.com/pulse/fearless-entrepreneurs hip-tackling-your-fears-christine/

Minasyan, A. (2024, November 11). AI Business Plan Generator Examples: demos, insights, and tips. *10Web - Build & Host Your WordPress Website*. https://10web.i o/blog/ai-business-plan-generators/

Mohan, P. R. (2023, September 10). *5 AI tools for planning your Budget*. https://w ww.linkedin.com/pulse/5-ai-tools-planning-your-budget-priya-ranjani-mohan/

monday.com. (n.d.). *Customizable Marketing Templates | Monday.com*. https://monday.com/lp/templates/marketing?cq_src=google_ads&cq_cmp=2095 2043111&cq_term=digital%20marketing%20strategy%20template&cq_plac=&cq _net=g&cq_plt=gp&utm_medium=cpc&utm_source=adwordssearch&utm_cam paign=ww2-en-prm-workos-marketer-marketing_templates-h-search-desktop-core -aw&utm_keyword=digital%20marketing%20strategy%20template&utm_match_ type=e&cluster=marketing&subcluster=marketing_plan&ati=&utm_adgroup=m arketing%20strategy%20template&utm_banner=687842504811&gad_source=1&

gclid=CjwKCAiA3JCvBhA8EiwA4kujZo4V-dvWPIe2bAV9oWnxiLtL1CjwoBU
vz-eWAxVnEFqloOR3VhqPlxoCFugQAvD_BwE

Monster.com. (2021, November 10). *7 Small business hiring Strategies | Monster.co
m*. https://hiring.monster.com/resources/small-business-hiring/hiring-process/hi
ring-strategies/

Morley, K., & Morley, K. (2024, August 14). *10 Best AI personalization tools for
websites, apps, email, and more*. Insider. https://useinsider.com/ai-personalization
-tools/

Mullinix, B. (2023, June 2). *How AI makes Forecasting Better for your startup*. http
s://www.zeni.ai/blog/how-ai-makes-forecasting-better

Mutua, M. (2024, September 16). *11 Companies That Are Killing It with Their
Digital Marketing Campaigns*. Convince & Convert. https://www.convinceand
convert.com/digital-marketing/killing-it-with-digital-marketing-campaigns/

Narain, A. (2023, November 7). *How Generative AI transforms fundraising*. Spice-
works Inc. https://www.spiceworks.com/tech/artificial-intelligence/guest-article/
generative-ai-in-fundraising/amp/

Newberry, C. (2024, November 12). *What is social media analytics? The 2024 guide
for marketers*. Social Media Marketing & Management Dashboard. https://blog.h
ootsuite.com/what-is-social-media-analytics/

NI Business Info. (n.d.). *Advantages and disadvantages of starting a business from
home | nibusinessinfo.co.uk*. https://www.nibusinessinfo.co.uk/content/advantage
s-and-disadvantages-starting-business-home

Ocasio, N. (2024, February 26). *AI tools for Business: 15 of the best*. Small Business
Trends. https://smallbiztrends.com/2024/02/ai-tools-for-business.html

Oetting, J. (2024, April 30). 28 Tools & Resources for Conducting Market Research.
HubSpot. https://blog.hubspot.com/marketing/market-research-tools-resources

Oluwatoni, O., & Oluwatoni, O. (2024, October 2). *14 Best AI Business Plan Generators (Free and Paid) in 2024*. Visme Blog. https://visme.co/blog/ai-business-plan/

Online marketing strategies for increasing sales revenues of small retail businesses. (2018). Walden University ScholarWorks. https://scholarworks.waldenu.edu/cgi/viewcontent.cgi?article=7175&context=dissertations

Orion Innovation. (2024, September 19). *Tax transformation for a Gobal enterprise.* https://www.orioninc.com/case-studies/tax-transformation/

Osman, M. (2024, July 22). Overcoming Your Fear of Failure as an Entrepreneur. *HubSpot.* https://blog.hubspot.com/the-hustle/fear-of-failure

P, P. (2024, April 9). *How to create an SEO-Friendly Website: 14 tips for Long-Term Organic Growth.* Hostinger Tutorials. https://www.hostinger.ph/tutorials/seo-friendly-website

Panel, E. (2023, March 16). 15 Ways Businesses can Keep up with Trends in the tech world. *Newsweek.* https://www.newsweek.com/15-ways-businesses-can-keep-trends-tech-world-1787815

Pec, T. (2022, September 6). *Why Businesses And Brands Need To Be Taking Advantage Of Social Media.* Forbes. https://www.forbes.com/sites/forbesagencycouncil/2022/09/06/why-businesses-and-brands-need-to-be-taking-advantage-of-social-media/?sh=26809f27216c

Peckover, T. (2024, October 2). *The 8 Best Brand Communities and Why They're Successful.* Loyalty & Reward Program Insights From Smile.io. https://blog.smile.io/8-best-brand-communities/

Perell, K. (2020, July 16). *5 Fears all entrepreneurs face (and how to conquer them).* Entrepreneur. https://www.entrepreneur.com/leadership/5-fears-all-entrepreneurs-face-and-how-to-conquer-them/353219

Petrat, P. (2024, October 22). *Why market research is important.* Cint™ | the World's Largest Research Marketplace. https://www.cint.com/blog/why-market-research-is-important

Pgadmin. (2022, October 26). *PlanGuru | Business Budgeting Software, Business Planning Software.* PlanGuru. https://www.planguru.com/

Pratt, M. K. (2024a, June 11). *Top 12 machine learning use cases and business applications*. Search Enterprise AI. https://www.techtarget.com/searchenterpriseai/feature/10-common-uses-for-machine-learning-applications-in-business

Pratt, M. K. (2024b, August 6). *12 key benefits of AI for business*. Search Enterprise AI. https://www.techtarget.com/searchenterpriseai/feature/6-key-benefits-of-AI-for-business

PricewaterhouseCoopers. (n.d.). *Generative AI in tax: 5 essential insights for leaders*. PwC. https://www.pwc.com/us/en/tech-effect/ai-analytics/generative-ai-insights-for-tax-leaders.html

Pros and Cons of a Home-Based Business vs. Brick and Mortar Business. (2021, May 26). Accion Opportunity Fund. https://aofund.org/resource/pros-and-cons-home-based-business-vs-brick-and-mortar-business/

Quantilope. (2024, November 22). 10 AI Market Research Tools & How To Use Them. *Quantilope*. https://www.quantilope.com/resources/best-ai-market-research-tools

Quora. (2019, October 31). Why is scaling so important in business? *Forbes*. https://www.forbes.com/sites/quora/2019/10/31/why-is-scaling-so-important-in-business/

Rajagopalan, R. (2024, November 20). *10 Examples of artificial intelligence in business*. University of San Diego Online Degrees. https://onlinedegrees.sandiego.edu/artificial-intelligence-business/

Renuka. (2021, March 1). *My guide to Champaner – the ancient city of Gujarat - Voyager for life*. Voyager for Life. https://www.renuka-voyagerforlife.com/2019/09/my-guide-to-champaner-the-ancient-city-of-gujarat.html

Reporter, G. S. (2022, September 30). Glossary of business terms - A to Z. *The Guardian*. https://www.theguardian.com/business/glossary-business-terms-a-z-jargon

Resilience and adaptability are key to navigating today's world. Here's why. (2024, September 10). World Economic Forum. https://www.weforum.org/agenda/2024/01/resilience-adaptability-key-navigating/

Revnuu. (2023, August 9). *The Role of Artificial Intelligence in Marketing: Enhancing Decision-making with AI-Driven Insights.* https://www.linkedin.com/pulse/role-artificial-intelligence-marketing-enhancing-decision-making/

Riddall, J. (2024, April 4). *35 Content marketing Statistics You should know.* Search Engine Journal. https://www.searchenginejournal.com/content-marketing-statistics-you-should-know/507173/

Risk assessment: process, tools, & techniques | SafetyCulture. (2024, September 12). SafetyCulture. https://safetyculture.com/topics/risk-assessment/

Robinson, B. (2024, April 4). *9 Bookkeeping basics Every bookkeeper needs.* Bookkeepers.com. https://bookkeepers.com/bookkeeping-basics/

rob.llewellyn@cxotransform.com. (2024, May 7). AI for Business - 30 case studies that led to competitive advantage. *Digital Transformation Skills.* https://digitaltransformationskills.com/ai-for-business/

Roman, M. (2024, June 10). *The 8 best AI tools for small Business.* Timeular. https://timeular.com/blog/best-ai-tools-small-business/

Sachdeva, A. (2023, February 7). *5 market research tools to help you research faster.* GapScout. https://gapscout.com/blog/market-research-tools/

Sajid, H. (2024, April 23). *The Intersection of AI across 6 major industries: Exploring latest AI applications from business perspective.* Unite.AI. https://www.unite.ai/the-intersection-of-ai-across-6-major-industries-exploring-latest-ai-applications-from-business-perspective/

Salah, H. (2023, May 7). *Blockchain Technology: a transformative force for all industries!* https://www.linkedin.com/pulse/blockchain-technology-transformative-force-all-industries-salah/

Santa Clara University. (n.d.). *Business Terms Glossary - My own Business Institute - Learn how to start a business*. https://www.scu.edu/mobi/resources--tools/busines s-terms-glossary/

Schooley, S. (2024, October 3). *Pros and cons of forming a corporation*. Business News Daily. https://www.businessnewsdaily.com/15805-corporation-advantages-and-d isadvantages.html

Schramade, W. & Erasmus Platform for Sustainable Value Creation. (2019). Mc-Donald's: a sustainable finance case study. In *Erasmus Platform for Sustainable Value Creation* [Journal-article]. https://www.rsm.nl/fileadmin/Faculty-Research /Centres/EPSVC/Case_study_sustainable_finance_McDonalds.pdf

Schramm, B. (2023, July 12). *20 Financial metrics Every business should track - Finmark*. Finmark. https://finmark.com/financial-metrics/

Scott-Briggs, A. (2020, October 6). *10 popular online technology forums for tech discussions*. TechBullion. https://techbullion.com/10-popular-online-technology -forums-for-tech-discussions/

Scout, H. (n.d.). *AI Customer Support Software: The 10 Best Tools for 2025 - Help Scout*. Help Scout. https://www.helpscout.com/blog/ai-customer-support-softwa re/

SentiOne. (2023, September 20). *Revolutionizing marketing: Inspiring AI Success Stories*. https://www.linkedin.com/pulse/revolutionizing-marketing-inspiring-ai-s uccess-stories-sentione/

Set goals for your business. (2024, July 11). Australian Government Business. https ://business.gov.au/planning/business-plans/set-goals-for-your-business

Shabalin, D. (2024, November 7). *Business Startup Checklist | MyCompanyWorks*. MyCompanyWorks. https://www.mycompanyworks.com/checklist.htm

Shad, A. A. (2024, September 15). *Feedback Analysis: analyzing quantitative and qualitative data*. Thoughts About Product Adoption, User Onboarding and Good UX | Userpilot Blog. https://userpilot.com/blog/feedback-analysis/

Shah, H. (2024, June 3). *Advantages of Artificial Intelligence (AI) for Your Business (2024 Updated).* Prismetric. https://www.prismetric.com/benefits-of-ai-for-business/

Singh, S. (2024, October 30). Improving Operational Efficiency for your business: A playbook for 2024. *Scribe.* https://scribehow.com/library/operational-efficiency

Siu, E. (2024, April 5). *How to implement AI in your business: A Step-by-Step guide.* Single Grain. https://www.singlegrain.com/blog/how-to-implement-ai-in-my-business/

Skillabilly. (2024, January 28). *Building resilience: Strategies for adapting to technological changes.* https://www.skillabilly.com/building-resilience-strategies-for-adapting-to-technological-changes/

Small business compliance checklist. (n.d.). Always Designing for People (ADP). https://www.adp.com/-/media/adp/resourcehub/pdf/sbs-fy20-compliance-checklist.pdf?rev=707e97e0c8b1430f81b900f011a30120

Small business website design: 8 tips for creating a website | Mailchimp. (n.d.) . Mailchimp. https://mailchimp.com/resources/small-business-website-design-tips

Solutions, V. (n.d.). *Vena Insights - Get secure, powerful & strategic insights | Vena Solutions.* https://www.venasolutions.com/platform/microsoft/insights

Solutions, V. (2024, June 17). The 9 Best AI Tools for Finance & FP&A (2024) - Vena. *Vena Solutions.* https://www.venasolutions.com/blog/best-ai-tools

SPD Technology. (n.d.). *AI-Powered Customer Behavior Prediction for eCommerce | SPD Technology.* https://spd.tech/artificial-intelligence/ai-for-customer-behavior-analysis/

Srmcp, T. R. M. C. F. (2023, March 11). *The top 10 tips for risk managers: Risk management.* https://www.linkedin.com/pulse/top-10-tips-risk-managers-management-tony-ridley-msc-csyp-msyi

Startup financing. (n.d.). The Hartford. https://www.thehartford.com/business-insurance/strategy/startup/money

Statista. (2024, November 5). *Worldwide digital population 2024.* https://www.statista.com/statistics/617136/digital-population-worldwide/#:~:text =Worldwide%20digital%20population%202024&text=As%20of%20July%202024 %2C%20there,population%2C%20were%20social%20media%20users.

Stay legally compliant. (n.d.). U.S. Small Business Administration. https://www.s ba.gov/business-guide/manage-your-business/stay-legally-compliant

St-Jean, E. (2023, October 23). *12 ways to create a continuous learning culture.* Search HR Software. https://www.techtarget.com/searchhrsoftware/feature/4-ways-to-c reate-a-continuous-learning-culture

Sustainable Cost Management: Balancing Sustainability and Cost Management Strategies. (2024, June 4). Faster Capi- tal. https://fastercapital.com/content/Sustainable-Cost-Management--Balancing -Sustainability-and-Cost-Management-Strategies.html

Sydle. (2024, January 11). *Business agility: What is it and how can it help you?* Blog SYDLE. https://www.sydle.com/blog/business-agility-what-is-it-63359b511770c 5640cf3b03b

Talent, A. (2023, September 28). *Unlocking Success: The importance of a Well-DEsigned Website for Artists, Brands, and businesses.* AMP Tal- ent. https://amptalent.com/learning_centers/unlocking-success-the-importance -of-a-well-designed-website-for-artists-brands-and-businesses/

Tax transformation with cloud ERP. (n.d.). Deloitte United States. https://www2.deloitte.com/us/en/blog/deloitte-on-cloud-blog/2023/tax-t ransformation-with-cloud-ERP.html

Taxology. (2023, March 8). *Digital transformation in accounting Firms: Benefits and challenges.* https://www.linkedin.com/pulse/digital-transformation-accounti ng-firms-benefits-challenges/

Taylor, C. (2023, October 5). How artificial intelligence is helping today's small businesses. *Forbes.* https://www.forbes.com/sites/charlesrtaylor/2023/08/09/how -artificial-intelligence-is-helping-todays-small-businesses/?sh=2aca2db71a48

Team, A., & Team, A. (2023a, May 30). *Predicting Customer Behavior with the Power of AI Marketing Tools*. AIContentfy. https://aicontentfy.com/en/blog/predicting -customer-behavior-with-power-of-ai-marketing-tools

Team, A., & Team, A. (2023b, June 30). *How to overcome fear and start your own business*. AIContentfy. https://aicontentfy.com/en/blog/how-to-overcome-fear-a nd-start-own-business

Team, A., & Team, A. (2023c, July 5). *The Beginner's Guide to understanding SEO Tools*. AIContentfy. https://aicontentfy.com/en/blog/beginners-guide-to-underst anding-seo-tools

Team, A., & Team, A. (2023d, November 6). *From Dreamers to Achievers: Stories of Entrepreneurship success*. AIContentfy. https://aicontentfy.com/en/blog/from-dre amers-to-achievers-stories-of-entrepreneurship-success

Team, C. S. (2018, June 26). Top 10 Federal Tax Compliance Issues for Businesses: Serving clients since 202. *CFO Selections*. https://www.cfoselections.com/perspect ive/top-10-federal-tax-compliance-issues-for-businesses

Team, S. (2024, November 11). Digital Marketing Case studies for small business- es. *SocialSellinator*. https://www.socialsellinator.com/social-selling-blog/digital-m arketing-case-studies-for-small-businesses

Team, W. (n.d.). *Why is web design important?* WebFX. https://www.webfx.com/ web-design/learn/why-is-web-design-important/

Team, W. (2023, October 5). *Scaling for Growth: Strategies for Successful Expansion*. Blog Wrike. https://www.wrike.com/blog/scaling-for-successful-growth/

TechAhead. (2024, August 16). *Top 25 Fintech AI use cases | TechAhead*. https://w ww.techaheadcorp.com/blog/top-25-fintech-ai-use-cases/

Technologies, B. (2024, November 14). *5 Benefits of AI in Inventory Management: Key Insights*. Binmile - Software Development Company. https://binmile.com/bl og/ai-inventory-management/

Technology, P. (2023, June 14). *AI: The Game-Changer for Small Businesses.* https ://www.linkedin.com/pulse/ai-game-changer-small-businesses-pulse-tech/

The How of Business Podcast. (2024, November 18). *Overcoming Fear to Grow Your Small Business with Ruth Soukup.* The How of Business Podcast & Resources. https://www.thehowofbusiness.com/episode-255-ruth-soukup/

The power of AI: What accounting and tax professionals need to know. (2024, July 2). Wolters Kluwer. https://www.wolterskluwer.com/en/expert-insights/the-power-o f-ai

The rise of Sustainable Finance: green investing, ESG and impact on finance careers. (2001, April 21). *William & Mary.* https://online.mason.wm.edu/blog/the-rise -of-sustainable-finance

The role of artificial intelligence in personalized marketing. (n.d.). https://abmatic. ai/blog/role-of-artificial-intelligence-in-personalized-marketing

The Top 5 Benefits of Adopting an AI-first Mindset in Business (and how to get employ- ees on board). (n.d.). https://www.launchconsulting.com/posts/the-top-5-benefits -of-adopting-an-ai-first-mindset-in-business-and-how-to-get-employees-on-board

The Unquestionable Benefits of AI in Accounting & Finance for 2024. (2023, Decem- ber 14). Quantic School of Business and Technology. https://quantic.edu/blog/2 023/03/20/artificial-intelligence-in-accounting-and-finance/

The Upwork Team. (2024, August 23). *Top 9 AI Tools for Finance Professionals: Discover 9 AI tools for finance professionals and how AI enhances financial services, from fraud detection to automated investing and tax help.* Upwork. https://www.u pwork.com/resources/ai-finance-tools

Thiemann, M. (2021, February 4). *Why is agility so important to the success of companies?* Forbes. https://www.forbes.com/sites/forbescoachescouncil/2021/02 /04/why-is-agility-so-important-to-the-success-of-companies/?sh=13c02f486f29

Thirteen essential tips for pitching to venture capitalists | Stripe. (2022, October 6). https://stripe.com/resources/more/pitching-venture-capitalists

Thompson, C. (2024, February 14). The role of artificial intelligence in cybersecurity. *Meriplex.* https://meriplex.com/the-role-of-artificial-intelligence-in-cybersecurity

Thompson, J. (2024, August 22). *Starting a business from home: The Ultimate checklist.* business.com. https://www.business.com/articles/starting-a-business-from-home-the-ultimate-checklist/

Todoros, O., & Todoros, O. (2024, September 3). *Why Digital Transformation is Essential for Accountants and CPA.* Spike. https://www.spikenow.com/blog/productivity/why-digital-transformation-is-essential-for-accountants-and-cpas-in-2023/

Top 10 Tax Compliance Pitfalls to avoid in 2024. (2023, December 19). Fonoa. https://www.fonoa.com/blog/top-10-tax-compliance-pitfalls-to-avoid-in-2024

TopAI.tools. (n.d.). AI Tax Calculator - Top AI Tools. https://topai.tools/s/AI-tax-calculator

Transforming Financial Planning in Food and Beverage: A Growth Case Study - 8020 consulting posts. (n.d.). https://8020consulting.com/food-beverage-financial-transformation-case-study/

Turnbull, A. (2020, February 6). *How I overcame one of my deepest fears as an entrepreneur | Groove Blog.* Groove Blog. https://www.groovehq.com/blog/overcoming-fear-as-an-entrepreneur

Twin, A. (2024, June 18). *What is a sole proprietorship?* Investopedia. https://www.investopedia.com/terms/s/soleproprietorship.asp

Ueland, S. (2023, February 23). 11 Outstanding Digital Media Campaigns from 2021. *Practical Ecommerce.* https://www.practicalecommerce.com/11-outstanding-digital-media-campaigns-from-2021

Uzialko, A. (2024, August 27). *How artificial intelligence will transform businesses.* Business News Daily. https://www.businessnewsdaily.com/9402-artificial-intelligence-business-trends.html

Vasilchenko, A. (2024a, November 1). *TOP 12 Machine Learning Technology Trends to Impact Business in 2024*. MobiDev. https://mobidev.biz/blog/future-machine-l earning-trends-impact-business

Vasilchenko, A. (2024b, November 6). *TOP 10 artificial intelligence trends that will make a big difference in business in 2024*. MobiDev. https://mobidev.biz/blog/fut ure-artificial-intelligence-technology-ai-trends

Vinton, P. (2024, July 29). *Navigating the data Landscape in 2024: 2 Key Trends to Watch*. Analytics8. https://www.analytics8.com/blog/top-trends-in-data-and-ana lytics/

Virtualinfocom. (2023, July 28). *Crafting a compelling pitch deck for your AI startup to secure funding*. https://www.linkedin.com/pulse/crafting-compelling-pitch-dec k-your-ai-startup-secure-funding/

Volopay. (2024, November 7). 7 reasons Why business budgets Fail | Volopay. *Volopay*. https://www.volopay.com/blog/why-do-business-budgets-fail/

Vzhuk. (2023, December 19). *The 4 Steps to Building an Effective AI Strategy | Stanford Online*. Stanford Online. https://online.stanford.edu/4-steps-building-ef fective-ai-strategy

Wavelaunch, & Wavelaunch. (2023, May 8). *7 Innovative ways to fund your startup*. Wavelaunch VC. https://wavelaunch.org/7-innovative-ways-to-fund-your-startup/

Weller, J. (2024, September 9). Simple business plan templates. *Smartsheet*. https: //www.smartsheet.com/content/simple-business-plan-templates

Westwater, S. (2023a, November 20). AI Marketing Case Study: Discover Success Stories and Cutting-Edge Strategies. *Pragmatic*. https://www.pragmatic.digital/bl og/ai-marketing-case-study-successful-campaigns

Westwater, S. (2023b, November 27). *AI Marketing Case Studies – Discover success Stories and Cutting-Edge Strategies*. https://www.linkedin.com/pulse/ai-marketin g-case-studies-discover-success-stories-scot-westwater-ag4ic

What are the financial metrics that a startup must track. (n.d.). InetSoft. https://www.inetsoft.com/business/bi/financial-metrics-startups-must-track/

What are the fundamentals of digital marketing? (2024, November 7). SNHU. https://www.snhu.edu/about-us/newsroom/business/what-are-the-fundamentals-of-digital-marketing

What is crowdfunding? Here are four types to know | Stripe. (2024, May 7). https://stripe.com/resources/more/four-types-of-crowdfunding-for-startups-and-how-to-choose-one

Whelan, T. (2017, June 1). *The Comprehensive Business Case for Sustainability.* Harvard Business Review. https://hbr.org/2016/10/the-comprehensive-business-case-for-sustainability

Why is budgeting important in business? 5 reasons. (2022, July 6). Business Insights Blog. https://online.hbs.edu/blog/post/importance-of-budgeting-in-business

Williams, M. (2023, June 14). *ENGAGING YOUR AUDIENCE THROUGH AUTHENTIC SOCIAL MEDIA COMMUNICATION.* https://www.linkedin.com/pulse/engaging-your-audience-through-authentic-social-media-mandy-williams/

wiseAdvizor. (2023, December 5). *Real-life Examples: Successful Startups that Secured Funding.* https://www.linkedin.com/pulse/real-life-examples-successful-startups-secured-funding-wiseadvizor-pe39f/

Wood, M. (n.d.). *10 Financial Tools Your Small Business Can't Live Without.* allBusiness: Your Small Business Advantage.

WordStream. (2023, November 13). *What is PPC? Learn the basics of Pay-Per-Click marketing.* https://www.wordstream.com/ppc

Workspace. (2011, September 5). *Glossary of business terminology.* Workspace ®. https://www.workspace.co.uk/content-hub/business-insight/glossary-of-business-terminology

Yoon, D. (n.d.). *11 Examples of continuous improvement companies | KaiNexus.* https://blog.kainexus.com/continuous-improvement-companies

York, A. (2024a, July 10). *10 best AI tools for customer Service to elevate your support.* ClickUp. https://clickup.com/blog/ai-tools-for-customer-service/

York, A. (2024b, August 23). *10 Best AI Tools for Accounting & Finance in 2024.* ClickUp. https://clickup.com/blog/ai-tools-for-accounting/

Your business needs to predict future trends. How can you get the most accurate results? (2024, January 26). https://www.linkedin.com/advice/0/your-business-needs-predict-future-trends-w3zef

Yuen, M. (2024, April 11). *Consumers worldwide prefer searching online over in-store for electronics, clothes, and other select categories.* EMARKETER. https://www.emarketer.com/content/consumers-search-products-online-over-in-store

Zenger News. (2024, June 3). Small businesses and their CEOS are starting to find success with AI. *Forbes.* https://www.forbes.com/sites/zengernews/2023/08/26/small-businesses-and-their-ceos-are-starting-to-find-success-with-ai/?sh=58d0209f15d6

Zeni. (n.d.). *Zeni: The #1 AI Bookkeeping Software | Automated Accounting.* https://www.zeni.ai/blog/ai-bookkeeping

Zerkalenkov, Z. (2024, January 8). *Brand Identity: What it is and how to create a strong one.* Semrush Blog. https://www.semrush.com/blog/build-brand-identity/

Zharovskikh, A. (2023, December 12). *Today in focus: ad spend optimization with artificial intelligence.* InData Labs. https://indatalabs.com/blog/ad-spend-optimization-with-ai

www.ingramcontent.com/pod-product-compliance
Lightning Source LLC
Chambersburg PA
CBHW071413210326
41597CB00020B/3482